TRANSFORMING
TEAMS

Develop yourself and your team
Transform your results!

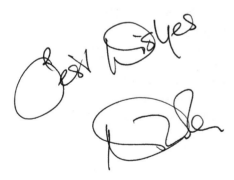

Nicola McHale

Transforming Teams

First published in 2011 by

Ecademy Press

48 St Vincent Drive, St Albans, Hertfordshire, AL1 5SJ

info@ecademy-press.com www.ecademy-press.com

Printed and Bound by Lightning Source in the UK and USA

Set by Charlotte Mouncey

Printed on acid-free paper from managed forests. This book is printed on demand, so no copies will be remaindered or pulped.

ISBN 978-1-907722-37-0

The right of Nicola McHale to be identified as the author of this work has been asserted in accordance with sections 77 and 78 of the Copyright Designs and Patents Act 1988.

A CIP catalogue record for this book is available from the British Library.

Dedications

For my children, Hannah and Alex – without you I would not be who I am today – thank you for facing the challenges and growing from them. You are great leaders and always will be.

For Karen – we have shared an amazing journey – thank you for all your love, support and friendship. You are the best friend anyone could have – thank you for always being there for me.

For Gavin, my husband – thank you for always being there for me and loving me for who I am.

To my parents who gave me the special gifts of love and the freedom to be myself. They let me develop, have fun and challenge myself along the way and taught me how important it is to never ever give up - thank you.

Acknowledgements

I would like to take this opportunity to thank the following people who have all contributed so much to my life and work.

Every client and every leader, their teams and every individual I have trained and coached over the last 25 years – even the ones who were the most difficult. You have challenged me, trusted me, stretched me and allowed me to work closely with you to transform yourselves and then given that gift to your teams. It has been an amazing experience. Without you this book would not be full of true experiences, examples and practical tips and tools that enabled you.

To the most inspirational woman I know – my Mum-in-law Elizabeth. Your determination, your positive attitude and your integrity are an inspiration and you will always be one of my greatest mentors. Thank you for always being there for me and being a great Mum after I lost my own.

To my family and true friends who nurture, challenge and explore life with me. Let us always have fun.

To Lucy for her patience as she helped me with my lack of PC skills – your skills make it look easy.

To Dylan for all his fantastic illustrations to bring alive the meaning of the book.

Contents

Introduction   9

PART ONE   13

Chapter One   Be Yourself   14

Chapter Two   Know your Strengths   34

Chapter Three   Know your Vision   48

Chapter Four   Know Your Impact   62

PART TWO   83

Chapter One   Know Your Team   84

Chapter Two   Build the Trust   99

Chapter Three   Create a Shared Vision   116

Chapter Four   Manage Conflict   132

PART THREE   159

Chapter One   Plan for Success   160

Chapter Two   Set ALL Targets   171

Chapter Three   Create a Performance Culture   180

Chapter Four   Celebrate Success   191

References   199

About the Author   201

Introduction

After more than 20 years building culturally diverse teams across the world in huge multi-nationals, I wanted to show you how you can do this in your team, in your organisation, with some tried and tested interventions.

This is a practical guide for the new leader, for a leader who has challenges in their team, whose team may be failing or underperforming or perhaps does not really want to be a leader but has found themselves with a team. It will also be useful for people who are forming their own businesses and want to design how they operate from the start – or perhaps a project team coming together for a short time and who have to work quickly together.

What would it be like if you knew how to build a great team where:

- Everyone was motivated

- Everyone was succeeding

- Everyone was using their strengths

- Everyone was developing

- Everyone was achieving

- Everyone talked about how great it was to be in this team

- People wanted to come and join your team

- People talked about how great a leader you were years afterwards

My aim is to help every leader to achieve this with my guide – the art and science to transforming a team.

'Great leaders are trained – not born'

Dr Paul Hersey

With my experience and knowledge, I have probably met every issue a leader can have, every challenge a team could face and every reason why a team fails. Over the years, I have designed some great interventions which are easy to implement, practical to employ and fun to do.

We are not taught how to be great leaders; we usually learn by experience. Often we will make big mistakes and regret later. I want you to avoid this and take some quick and simple steps early so that you don't fail.

I will share experiences, provide anecdotes and examples to bring the exercises to life. You can complete these exercises with your teams at any time.

I have separated the book into three parts:

Part One starts with you. Great teams are as a result of having a great leader. In this section I ask you to think deeply about yourself as a leader. What is your leadership personality?

It is not about being someone you are not; it is about maximising who you are and your potential.

It is about ensuring you do not stop yourself. It is about being truly honest with yourself.

It is about bringing your leadership alive so that you can have impact, motivate and inspire your people.

You may want to try and avoid this part but if you do you could fail.

It provides you with Coaching Moments and many hints and tips about how you can prepare yourself for leadership and for bringing your teams together.

Part Two is about building your team and starting the process of getting to know them. Great teams know one another and know their leader. They have a shared purpose, vision and values. This part shows you 'how' to create a vibrant, motivated team – a team which is working together to ensure success.

Part Three is about how you bring everything together to ensure you achieve your targets and results.

Some of you will want to start here, I am sure, and that is fine – but if you have not completed the rest, you run the risk of failing early on.

It is about becoming very clear about what the targets are and how you need to focus your energy on what you can achieve rather than what you are not doing well.

Each part has Coaching Moments for both you, the leader, and for the team.

Each chapter has a summary so that you can fast-track.

The guide is about how you can become a great leader, create a great team and achieve great results.

It is important to remember that the guide provides deep insights; however you do not need a psychology degree to use it or transform a team. Just remember to be mindful of the people around you, and what their life has given them is not always what you think it has.

It can be a very lonely place being a leader, with no one to turn to for advice or support. This guide will help you when times are tough. It will teach you how to self-coach.

It is also about how you can become an authentic leader in all areas of your life – at home as well as at work. You can use everything in this guide to make your life better and more worthwhile at home. The beauty is in the art of keeping it simple but meaningful.

So read the book through, keep it with you, refer back to it and use it to help you develop yourself and your teams. Practise the exercises so that you are fully prepared.

.... and remember it all starts with you. Start now transforming yourself, your team and your results.

Being a great leader – the best your team has ever had – is the outcome of this book – my gift to you and everyone you 'touch' as you travel your life journey.

PART ONE

Transform Yourself

Chapter One

Be Yourself

Being the greatest leader you can be is what will make the difference to your career and your life.

I remember meeting one of my greatest leaders for the first time about 15 years ago; he was a young high-potential with a high IQ who had suddenly inherited a team because of his great results and successful delivery. He was in shock, concerned and anxious as he had had no leadership development. He felt he was great at the day job but not as a leader: 'How am I going to lead all these talented people?' So we started that journey to 'turn me' into a great leader. Now he is remembered throughout the organisations he has worked in as exactly that. They still talk about him now. He has enabled many others to become great leaders and they are continuing that, keeping his legacy alive. I saw him transform himself, transform his teams and achieve the most amazing results. He achieved success in the right way and he is remembered for 'how' he led his teams.

You are a leader in many areas of your life, not just at work. Leadership starts 'at home' with you. You are a leader as you lead yourself through your life. You are a leader at home and a leader at work, even if you do not have a team.

I have learned there is no perfect model of leadership. Everyone can be a great leader if they really want to. There are literally thousands of courses but most will be a waste of time. There have been, and are, some great leaders of our time – Mandela, Gandhi, Martin Luther King, Churchill – who have quite literally changed the world. They didn't go to business school to learn how to do it. They operated by knowing themselves, tapping into everything they had, having a vision and staying focused until they achieved it. They never gave up or made excuses or blamed others – they took responsibility, they motivated and inspired others and they were determined to succeed despite incredible obstacles in their way.

Knowing and understanding yourself is a vital part of leadership and one that many leaders assume they do. However, in my experience so many try to be someone else or try to hide who they really are – is that you? You can and will be a great leader if you spend some time developing your leadership personality

As Steve Jobs, the late CEO of Apple Corporation said:

'Your time is limited so don't waste it living someone else's ... have the courage to follow your own heart and intuition.'

Building a successful team starts with you, so start by taking responsibility now for developing yourself to be the best leader you can be – it is up to you because it is not always easy and you will meet some hurdles along the way – just never give up.

There is no point trying to change the fundamentals of who you are – it is so much better to stop and think about you, what your strengths are, what your values are and what culture you want to create in your team.

So just for a moment stop and think: Who have been the greatest leaders in your life? Who has made the biggest positive impact on you and why? It may have been a teacher at school or a parent or someone who came into your life for a short while but left you with something very special that you still value today. What are those things you learned?

- Respect others e allow them to think / speak / say things.

- Think of a solution then go to the boss e discuss.

- Develop others to their full potential.

Just think back and take time to remember them. Acknowledge them if you can now! Even if you cannot physically do that, just take a moment to think about them and what they gave you because it's immeasurable and will stay with you all your life.

My mother was one of my greatest teachers. She was always positive, always determined to never give up and always made the best out of a bad situation. She taught me to be resilient, to look on the positive side of life and to enjoy the moment.

Up to the point when she died of cancer at a young age, she continued to live by those beliefs and they stay alive in me today as empowering beliefs – beliefs that drive many of my successful behaviours.

Conversely, I also took on the limiting belief that I would die at a young age. I chose to change that once I was aware of what I was doing – trying to do everything at a hundred miles an hour, making myself so stressed and tired which, in the end, would have caused serious illness, I believe. By changing that belief structure, I now believe I will live to a good age and be healthy and fit and my behaviours support that.

So let me say something personally to you before you start this journey of your development: no matter what the past has told you, you can and will be a great leader even if you are new to this or if you have had past failures. Now is different – I know that because you are ready and are open to learning how to be a great leader, which is why you are reading this book. The most important thing for you to do is use this guide to enable you to transform yourself and your teams – that way you will be a great leader.

So just for a moment now ...

Remember that leader who was one of your greatest teachers and start to think about how you would like to be described by one of your teams in years to come – just write down a few words here, we will use them later in this guide. Imagine your team is in another room discussing you in a few years time when you are moving on. What would you like them to say about you?

It is worth spending some quiet time reflecting on this because it will give you valuable information to help you – maybe take yourself somewhere special where you can be alone with yourself, with nothing else going on like your mobile phone or your emails. Just time for you.

- Empowering of others

- Sharer of information

- Professional in all she does.

Ensure that you are asking for what you want rather than what you do not want. The focus of your attention will come up in this book time and time again, so I just want to say 'be careful what you ask for as your mind will deliver it'. Your mind is your most powerful tool, however it can also be your own worst competitor and try to derail you when the 'negative self speak' is turned on.

Programme your mind to deliver what you want, not what you don't want. Have you heard this before: 'I don't want you to imagine there is a blue elephant sitting on your car now'? I suspect you have already formed that picture, haven't you? The brain finds it impossible to process negative words like 'don't'. Programme it with positive statements, for example, 'I will be a fantastic leader to my team/teams – the best they ever had and we will achieve great success together'.

Now you are starting to think about what's important to you as a leader and how you want to be perceived and that is very powerful because you are starting to create your vision of success.

There are eight levels of understanding that I use with leaders which it is vital to become clear on as you start your leadership journey to become a great leader. Take time with each level and write down a few notes to yourself.

Be The Best Leader You Can Be

Culture	When and where are you a great leader?
	What environment is present?
	What culture is present?
Behaviour	What do you do when you are leading at your best?
	What behaviours are present?
Strengths	What strengths are present?
	How do you use those strengths?
Beliefs	What do you believe to be true about you?
	What do you believe about others?
	What could stop you being a great leader?
Values	What is important to you as a leader?
	What values and principles are you operating by?
Vision	What is your vision of success as a leader?
Core Purpose	What is your purpose as a leader?
	What is your legacy?

By becoming clear on the above and working on these key areas as you develop yourself you will be creating your leadership personality – and that will make you unique.

There are many different types of leader and I have had the amazing experience of working with some of the most senior levels across the world and the most successful over the last 20 years.

What I know now is...

- They are all very different

- They are all unique

- They use their strengths – they know what they are great at

- They know their weaknesses or 'areas of development' and they are prepared to work on them

- They are highly self-aware

- They are prepared to change their behaviours

- They know what they can change and what they cannot change

- They are prepared to laugh at themselves and with their teams

- Some are introverted

- Some are extroverted

- Some are detailed, some are not

- Some are intuitive, some are not

- Some are logical and detached

- Some are organised and planned

- Some are flexible and unplanned

- all had integrity.

- all had a vision and all left their legacies.

Another great leader I have worked with is still remembered now for being truly amazing, and not just for the fact that she led a huge part of a blue-chip organisation – some 10,000 people – but because she made them feel special; she could spot potential and then she helped people realise it. She connected with everyone from the cleaner right through to her leadership team. She took the time to remember their names and what was going on in their lives. She provided support when they needed it and she stood up for them. She did not go to university but she did have the highest emotional intelligence which made the difference and made her one of the most successful leaders I have worked with.

They still remember her now, many years after she left, as being the one leader that made a difference to them. Many of them told me that she was pivotal to their success. That could be you.

First of all, though, we need to take a look at how you could stop yourself. Transforming leaders never let anything stop them, least of all themselves.

What could stop you?

Change your self-limiting beliefs and behaviours

Sometimes we collect feedback over the years from well-meaning leaders, parents, siblings, managers and situations we have experienced – all of which in the end can make us think that we are not, and never will be, a good leader. For example:

'You will never be a good leader'

'You're too shy to be a leader'

'You're too quiet – leaders are always gregarious'

'You are no good with people'

We collect our learning along the way; everything we have ever done is etched in our memory and stored deep within our unconscious minds. Our memory is like a huge database of knowledge and experience which we can tap into at any given moment – and you can too, if you let yourself!

The conscious mind occupies only about 2% of your total capacity. It takes in the information through your five senses: see, feel, hear, smell and taste. It then sorts the information, deleting it if it is not relevant or important to you (have you ever said something to someone and they totally ignored it?); generalising it if you have other information to compare it against (when you say things like 'that's typical of him, he always does that'); or distorting it to fit your beliefs and values (when you make meaning, assumptions or totally change the fact.) It is human behaviour, it will happen and you will do it – just know not all of it is helpful to you or your relationships or to becoming a great leader.

The unconscious mind stores all your beliefs (what you think is right and true for you), your values (your guiding principles), your knowledge and experiences, your vision and purpose (the reasons why you do what you do, what drives and motivates you) and your identity (your personality – who you are). It also stores everything that has ever happened so it's there for you when you need it.

So often we try and forget or 'bury' our past when in fact it has many treasures for us. A vital part of self-leadership is to take some time looking back along our life line and highlighting our learning and experiences. This is where and how our personality was shaped and developed. This is where you discovered your strengths and your uniqueness.

By doing this you will also start to see how and when you developed your self-limiting beliefs and behaviours. Remember you were not born with them; young children are free to be themselves, we just learn as we go along. Some experiences are helpful and supportive whilst others are not. So what made you who you are today?

Key Imprinting

0-7 years – think back to this time. What can you remember? It is a key time when many of our deepest core values are imbedded. It is the time when we have to venture out into the world to school and meet people from outside our family. What did you learn?

7-14 years – think back to this time. It is a time when we learn about ourselves in our social groups and how we fit into those groups. It is a time when we are making friends and when we are finding out what we are good at and what we are not so good at. What did you learn?

14-21 years – think back to that time. It is a time when we become much clearer about our strengths and weaknesses, when we have our first relationships, when we often make very strong friendships and when our academic abilities are confirmed. It's also a time when we leave home and find out how well-equipped we are to survive in the outside world alone. What did you learn?

By 21 we are ready – our values, beliefs and behaviours are embedded. We think we know what we are good at and what we are not good at.

Why is this important to know? Well, this is when you learned to be who you are. This is the time when you were 'led' by others – some good, some not so good. This is when you will have started to have feedback about yourself – some good, some not so good! Why is this important to being a transforming leader? Well, great leaders are highly self-aware, they know themselves, they have good self-control, they have great social awareness and brilliant relationship management. The good news is that you can develop these skills once you understand who you really are and how you could stop yourself – your life line will give you those gifts, no matter how tough it has been. There is always positive learning from every negative experience.

It is a powerful exercise to create your life line – just a simple one. Take the time and go somewhere private and quiet. Time for you. Take that time now.

Coaching Moment

Exercise

0 ——→ 7 ——→ 14 ——→21 ———————→ age now

Use as much space as you need. Take a small notepad.

Add the key positive experiences in one colour and what you learned from them. What values were embedded?

When were you successful? What are you proud of?

Add the challenging experiences in a different colour. What self-limiting beliefs did you take on then? What did you learn that was positive for you?

It is important to remember that your self-limiting beliefs will drive your behaviour and will cause you to fail and not reach your potential, and eventually possibly stop you being successful. You know now they were formed as a result of past experiences and are not necessarily true now. So exactly what are your self-limiting beliefs in relation to you becoming a transforming leader?

It is about just being you, knowing you are OK, knowing that you will make mistakes but knowing you will learn from them and do better next time.

Your limiting beliefs and behaviours can have a huge effect on your performance. A perfect example of someone causing their own failure was that of a senior vice-president I worked with who was asked to speak to 900 people at an industry conference – proud but terrified. We did a belief audit as he was so scared of the thought of presenting to his peers in the industry. We changed his self-limiting beliefs and replaced them with empowering beliefs. We worked on his extreme emotional reactions and changed them to more empowering emotions. He faced his fears, worked on them and practised in front of a camera until he was great. I saw him present and do an amazing job. That sounds easy but it wasn't; it took about three months to understand why he had such extreme responses and then change them. The root cause of this 'fear' came from his school experiences. Once we analysed those years, he was free to explore how to be a great presenter – today. He did it.

The important thing to learn is that you can do anything you want to as long as you are prepared to put in the effort to change and don't stop yourself with your negative thoughts.

Coaching Moment

So in terms of leadership – do a limiting belief audit now – what do you believe to be true about you becoming a transforming leader? What self-limiting beliefs do you have?

.

.

Once you have listed them ask yourself these questions:

What does 'it' feel like inside of you?

When did you first know that this was 'true' for you?

What value does this limiting belief support – if any?

If you carry on thinking this is true what will be the effect on your career?

Stop and think – take time on your own and look at your own answers.

What would be a more positive and empowering belief to believe instead?

When have you believed this before?

What does this belief 'feel' like?

What value/values does this empowering belief support?

If you carry on as if this is true then what will this belief do for your career?

How are you going to act differently now?

Take responsibility – it is up to you to use your time powerfully.

Think about what you can control and influence – and who and what you cannot influence. So many people waste enormous amounts of time on things they cannot change.

I remember working with the senior leaders in some now very successful National Health Service (NHS) Primary Care Trusts (PCT) when it had been announced that there would be huge changes and unprecedented cuts within the NHS – 50% were going to lose their jobs within two years!

No influence and no control; some got stuck and stayed in the denial and anger stage, not listening/ adding to rumours and gossip – wasting their time and embedding fear and anxiety throughout the organisation and in themselves. They couldn't change what was happening – those who stayed in this frame became part of the problem and stayed stuck. It is a waste of time staying in this mindset. You cannot change what you cannot control or influence.

Influence but no control – some started to think about whom they could influence to find other jobs but did not go that step further. This is an important frame of mind. Stopping and thinking about who and what you can influence is critical to success. Then be proactive.

Some took control and thought about what they could do, what and who they could influence. They became part of the solution. They were the ones who took action and found new jobs as they came up in the NHS and outside. They made their own success and they made their organisation more successful through transition.

There is always an answer to a problem at some level. Successful people never give up and they know that if they look hard enough they will find a solution.

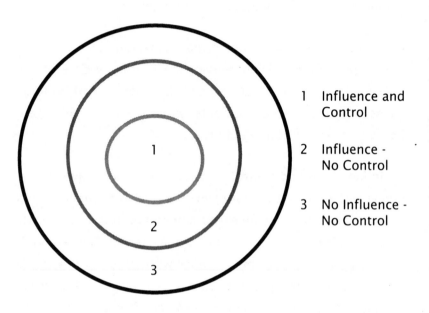

1 Influence and Control

2 Influence - No Control

3 No Influence - No Control

So stop and think now – in terms of 'becoming a transforming leader, transforming your team and achieving your results'. Take the inner circle. What/who can you control and influence?

.

.

.

.

Middle Circle - What/who can you influence but not control?

-
-
-
-
-

Outer Circle - What/who can you NOT control or influence?

-
-
-
-
-

Remember, don't stop yourself

You can be your biggest barrier, your toughest competitor, so get clear on:

- Your leadership personality – your vision and values

- Your life line – highs, lows and learnings

- Your self-limiting beliefs and behaviours

- What you can control and influence

- Who and what you can influence

- Develop your leadership skills

Build your emotional intelligence – emotional freedom

Sometimes we can feel extreme emotions connected to our limiting beliefs. Transforming leaders never let these stop them; they have a heightened emotional awareness. Some of them have experienced huge traumas, great fear and anxiety but still they survived them and went on to do great things to change our world. So if they can do it, so can we.

To have greater emotional control you need to clear yourself of any unproductive emotional responses. Sometimes we can regret our reactions afterwards – great leaders always act with integrity.

As an experienced leadership coach I have worked with senior leaders with many self-limiting beliefs and negative emotional responses. Here is an exercise I have created for changing emotional responses. Remember every emotion is there for a reason. NB: this is not an exercise to use for any traumas.

Coaching Moment

Think about any concerns or worries you may have in regard to being a great leader, building your team or achieving your results. Write them down.

Now think about the emotion that you feel – name it:

- Where is it located physically?

- What shape is it?

- What is the metaphor to describe it?

- What colour is it?

- Is it moving or still?

- What sound does it have? What is it saying?

Now ask yourself:

- What is its positive intention for you?

- What action does it want you to take?

- What else?

Continue until that emotion has subsided. Just continue the exercise until, eventually, it subsides and you will feel calm inside.

An emotional audit is important to do periodically so that you remain clear, and working with your emotions rather than avoiding them or ignoring them. I do my audit when I am flying on business when I have time on my own and the space to think about how I am feeling. Our emotions are there for a vital reason – the 'fight or flight' mechanism. They are there to look after us and keep us safe and very often we can feel them before we even know intellectually that something is wrong, but they all have a positive intention for us.

If you are feeling extreme emotions then you will need professional help.

Once you know yourself and you have learned from all your experiences (good and bad) then you can bring all that with you to enable yourself to become one of the greatest leaders your team have ever had. You are unique and we need to bring that uniqueness out.

Summary

1. What is your leadership legacy? How do you want to be remembered by your team?

2. What is your leadership personality?

    Be the greatest leader you can be

    Purpose

    Vision

    Values

    Beliefs

    Strengths

    Behaviour

    Culture

3. Create your life line – the highs and the lows.
    Know what you learned that was positive for you.

    0 – 7

    7 – 14

    14 – 21

4. Change your self-limiting beliefs.

5. Get clear on what you can control and influence.

6. Clear negative emotions.

7. Do an 'emotional freedom' exercise.

Chapter Two

Know Your Strengths

Great leaders use their strengths. They know what they are good at and they use those skills to create their success. They know that when they use their strengths their ways of thinking are better, their positive emotions are heightened, they are energised and their performance is exceptional.

Many organisations are now taking a 'strengths' approach – you can be ahead of the game by using yours to be a transforming leader.

There is compelling evidence that demonstrates that a strengths focus delivers huge business advantages and delivers measurable business returns:

- Increased revenues

- Reduced costs

- Customer engagement

- Improved morale and personal well-being

- Stress management

- Employee engagement

- Increased confidence

- Improved relationship management

- Higher productivity

- Inspiring transformational leadership

The business case for a strengths-focused approach is proven (supplied by Strengths Partnership 2010). There an increasing number of published studies showing all the above advantages. Here are some for those of you who may question this approach or who want more detail. I offer the following to emphasise the importance of a strengths focus as recognised by psychological research.

Higher Productivity, Better Financial Results and Reduced Turnover

Research suggests gratitude, positive emotion and engagement improve productivity, reduce turnover and boost profits. Other research shows measurable increases in happiness and bonding after people share success stories.

In a recent analysis of over 10,000 work units and over 300,000 employees in 51 companies, it was found that work units scoring above the median on the statement 'I have the opportunity to do what I do best every day' have a 38% higher probability of success on productivity measures and a 44% higher probability of success on customer loyalty and employee retention.

Source: Harter & Schmidt, 2002 -
Strengthscope Partnership

Inspiring, Transformational Leadership

Studies have found that leaders who exhibit more positive emotion and behaviour are more likely to be rated as demonstrating transformational leadership behaviours, including inspiring others and demonstrating more consideration and empathy for followers.

Leaders' expressions of positive emotions have been found to arouse positive emotions in others; followers tend to emulate their leaders' positive energy and enthusiasm. Similarly leaders' displays of negative emotion can cause followers to feel and display negative emotions, undermining morale and motivation.

Source: Barsade & Gibson, 2007 –
Strengthscope Partnership

Stronger Teamwork and Supportive Behaviour

In a research project undertaken at Toyota North American Parts Centre California involving over 400 employees on 54 work teams, a strengths-based team intervention with the objective of building effective work teams contributed a 6-9% increase in productivity per employee over a one-year period.

This was achieved against a backdrop of productivity improvements of less than 1% over the previous three years.

Researchers have also found that employees who experience positive moods at work are more likely to be helpful and supportive towards their colleagues. They are not only willing to put in extra effort to get their own job done to a higher standard, but are also more likely to help others out, going beyond the requirements of their job description.

Source: Connelly, 2002; Barsade & Gibson, 2007 –
Strengthscope Partnership

'The Gallup Organisation asked this question of 198,000 employees working in 7,939 companies: "At work do you have the opportunity to do what you do best every day?" We then compared the responses to the performance of the business units and discovered the following: When employees answered 'strongly agree' to this question, they were 50% more likely to work in business units with lower employee turnover, 38% more likely to work in more productive business units, and 44% more likely to work in business units with higher customer satisfaction scores. And over time those business units that increased the numbers of employees who strongly agreed saw comparable increases in productivity, customer loyalty, and employee retention. Whichever way you care to slice the data, the organisation whose employees feel that their strengths are used every day is more powerful and more robust.'

(Now Discover Your Strengths, Marcus Buckingham & Donald O Clifton, Free
Press Business, 2001)

'Years of research prove that individuals and teams playing to their strengths significantly out-perform those who don't in almost every business metric.'

(Marcus Buckingham, Management Guru and Author, 2009)

'The effective executive makes strengths productive. (S)he knows that one cannot build on weaknesses. To achieve results, one has to use all the available strengths – the strengths of associates, the strengths of the superior, and one's own strengths. These strengths are the true opportunities.'

(Peter Drucker, Management Guru and Author, 1967)

'Companies where the focus is on amplifying the positive attributes … rather than combating negatives … perform better financially and otherwise.'

(Bronwyn Fryer – Editor Harvard Business Review, 2004).

So – let's take some time thinking about your strengths and not your weaknesses.

To excel at leadership and to enjoy it, you need to understand your uniqueness – strengths are one of the important tools and they are already there – you just need to use them more and access them readily when you need them.

Go back to the exercise we did in Chapter One page 19 – Be the Best Leader you can Be. What strengths did you write down?

Write them here again:

-
-
-
-
-

So many leaders fail to acknowledge that they have huge strengths which will release their leadership potential, so don't be one of those. It's these strengths that will enable you to achieve success far quicker than working on your perceived 'failings'.

So the first step to remember is – 'you do have amazing strengths already'. Maybe you just don't know them yet, maybe you've never been told or maybe you focus too much on what you are not good at. Which are you?

Great leaders are brave. They seek out feedback, they want to know what they are doing well so they can do more of it, they want to know what they need to stop doing and want to know what they need to focus on developing. That way they can continue to grow. They are always curious.

They know their core strengths, they use them 80-90% of the time because they know that, when they do, their energy surges and they can make a difference very, very quickly – their performance is exceptional.

But of course sociologically we know that some of us are programmed differently. We can have had negative input and feedback; we can have had managers early on in our career (or even later) who have had the power to take our confidence away with very bad leadership behaviours.

Make a mental note to yourself now to never be remembered like that. There is a way to give and receive feedback later in this book (Part 3 Chapter 3 page 183) so that you empower and develop your people. A leader who gives powerful feedback to his/her people will always be remembered for having made a difference to them and treated them with respect and dignity whilst remaining honest.

As you now know, everything that has ever happened to us is stored in our unconscious mind and can be triggered at a moment's notice by just one look or remark. Just think now of your favourite toy as a child and picture it – remember playing with it? Just allow the memory to access it because it will very quickly. That is a great memory to keep. Maybe you still have that toy somewhere?

Remember the life line exercise, refresh yourself on that now – if you need to.

We know we have some negative memories which are connected to the tough times we have had and where our self-limiting behaviours and beliefs originate. So if you have had negative feedback from well-meaning parents, teachers, peers or 'friends' or managers that cause you to think that you don't have many leadership strengths – then think again. It is time to change all of that – we all have amazing strengths, we just need to find them and use them to develop our leadership potential.

One way to know what your team think your strengths are is to ask for feedback. There are two ways to do this. First, you could ask your company to administer a 360° feedback tool on your leadership capability or you can contact us at Vi International and we can do it for you. A 360° is where you ask your team, your peers, your leader and your critical stakeholders for feedback on your leadership capability.

Secondly you could run a 360° or a self-report to access your strengths. There are two which I recommend – the details are at the end of this Chapter page 46. A self-report is as it says – you answer the questions from your perspective only.

One of the leaders I have worked with in USA recently had their top three strengths as Strategic Mindedness, Common Sense and Results-Focused. However, they were not collaborating with their team or showing any empathy, nor were they interested in developing their team. The team was disfunctioning.

After strengths coaching, he was more aware how he could use his strengths to become a great leader even if he did not have 'traditional leadership strengths'. His team could learn from him how to stay focused on their results and how to stay focused on the future direction of the business, whilst he could learn from the team about how to be more empathetic and collaborative with them.

We started to think about his long-term goals for his leadership of the team and how he knew he would be successful – what results he would have achieved in terms of his leadership. Then I saw him change; he became more alive, more aware of what he was going to do. That made the biggest difference in the shortest time because he was using his core strengths and not his weaknesses.

So once you know what your cores strengths are, once you take the time to access and use the energy they bring, you will start to access a wealth of capabilities which you can use right now, and easily. That's when you will be 'at your best' all the time, everywhere, with everyone. Every time you are working with your strengths, you will feel very different from when using your 'weaknesses'. You will feel more energetic, lighter, more focused and relaxed, more determined and more confident. This feeling will radiate throughout your body – you will quite literally feel amazing and by the end of the day at work you will still feel fresh and motivated. What would that be like?

Here is an exercise to practise so that you can 'feel' the difference. Once you know that then you can access that feeling every time you need it.

Coaching Moment

Exercise – Access your Energy Strengths Surge

Just remember now a time when you were operating at your best, at your peak and go back to that time as if you were reliving it now. Take the time to experience it again. Remember it makes sense to use past positive experiences to help power us to success rather than the opposite.

So ask yourself what is happening? What can you see and hear? How does it feel when you know you are doing a fantastic job? What can you hear others saying? See everything around you again now. See what you can see, hear what you can hear; now hold on to that visualisation and feel the surge of energy that radiates throughout your body – let it happen. This is an important step so don't rush it. Really feel it, see it and hear yourself.

Especially important is to feel the feelings of where the energy surge is coming from. Where is it located in the body? Be specific. What does it feel like? Access that feeling and remember it so that you can use that energy surge to use your strengths.

Write down here what strengths you were using, what you did and how that felt.

.

.

.

I remember when I was working with a global team in Asia. Just imagine it now: ten people had flown in from around the world to be there for the week. It was a two-day event and it was a vital time in the team's development.

Day One went well, everyone contributed, everyone participated and, on the surface, everything was going OK but I knew, because of the pre-event interviews I had conducted, that there was deep resentment among two or three of them that wasn't surfacing – yet – but it did overnight, over dinner and into the next morning. I arrived fully prepared, not knowing what had happened during the previous late night chat. All flip charts and presentations were complete – until I was told what had happened literally five minutes before I was to go on stage! I had to delete everything on the agenda immediately and think quickly what to do. I tapped into my core strengths:

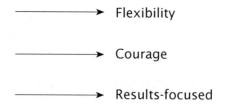

⟶ Flexibility

⟶ Courage

⟶ Results-focused

This allowed me to know that here was a great opportunity for a big breakthrough in the team dynamics. It was the time to go for it, encouraging them towards some brave conversations, having the one-to-one chats they needed to have and for them to begin the process of understanding one another, their different cultures, values and beliefs. I was determined and focused on every word and action. We had an amazing day where they talked about everything they needed to discuss. It was tough, it was scary, but they did it and it turned out to be the pivotal event of their new journey – which they still talk about now. They went on to be one of the most successful teams I have ever worked with and they are still achieving fantastic results even though their original leader moved on.

It could have been so different if I had been one of those facilitators who insisted on keeping to the agenda, who took control of the conversations, who did not listen to every word that was said and not said. The leader was amazing; he sat back and let it happen because he knew he could trust me and knew it all had to come out on to the table but in a facilitated 'safe' way.

Once you know your strengths and think back to times when you have used them, do the 'visualisation' exercise and get the 'strengths surge'– then you can use this energy when you need it the most. This next exercise will help you to get ready for any future challenge.

Coaching Moment

State Management

Think of a time in the future when you have to face a challenging situation – which of your strengths are needed? How can your strengths help you to be successful?

Take those strengths now and imagine you are in that future situation – visualise success, hear yourself operating in that experience using your strengths – go on, do it – you can if you allow yourself to. Then come back to now in your mind.

Now list what actions you need to take to get prepared:

.

.

.

It's vital to prepare like this for any really challenging situation – that's what successful people do.

Sportsmen and women do this before they go on the pitch, out on to the court or on to the fairway – so you can. Just watch them, it's clear to see. You will see them taking some time with themselves, changing their breathing patterns; often you will see them looking upwards, visualising success, they may have that 'lucky' routine to do. They will definitely be talking to themselves inside with clear mantras on what to do. Just watch them and concentrate on what it is they do.

Mine is: I take time alone or maybe just turning to a window. Looking out straight ahead, I visualise success. I push my breathing down, deep breathing, calm but energising from my toes upwards; then I say to myself 'I can do it'.

What is yours? Take some time to refine this process for yourself. There is no right one, just one that works for you.

Winning Strategies

We all have two or three winning strategies as a result of our strengths. These are normally formed in the first 21 years of life – what are yours? One of mine is to 'never ever give up' – part of it came from my Mum and seeing how she fought against the cancer, but it was there even before then. It was when I was about seven and it continued right throughout school. I was very competitive with myself and always wanted to win. It all came from wanting to please my parents, so I kept on practising my maths tables, my spelling, my running – everything I could. I never gave up! I know now that whatever life throws at me, and it has thrown some challenging stuff, I will never ever give up. I will keep searching for the answer.

So when did you learn your strengths? When did you use your winning strategies as you were growing up?

Because of these strengths it's these strategies which will ensure that you will be a great leader.

List them here – what are your top three strengths and your three winning strategies?

Strengths

- .

- .

- .

Winning strategies

- .

- .

- .

If you want to get even clearer about your unique strengths, as I said there are two great tools you can use.

Over my career I have worked with people and organisations that use both StrengthsFinder and Strengthscope – both are extremely useful to you as a leader and for your whole organisation. That way you can ensure you have the best people in the right roles so they can make the greatest difference to the success of the team/organisation.

You can put yourself to the test with www.strengthsfinder.com or you can complete a Personal or 360° Strengthscope with us at www.viinternational.com.

Summary

1. Ask for feedback from your team and do a 360°
    Leadership Inventory.

2. Do a strengths 360° – know your core strengths.

3. Access your strengths energy surge.

4. Practise your state management.

5. What are your winning strategies?

Chapter Three

Know Your Vision

By now you know more about who you are as a leader, your values, your strengths; a vital piece of the jigsaw is to create your leadership legacy, your vision, elicit your values and get clear about who you need to influence in order to achieve success. This separates you from others. Once that is known, then we will create your 'elevator pitch' so that you can communicate clearly what is important to you.

All our greatest leaders and our greatest sportsmen and women are ordinary people who have achieved the extraordinary. They all had a vision of success and they all worked hard until they achieved it.

In my experience, those leaders who spend time on this area achieve the buy-in of their teams much more speedily than others.

Every leader I have worked with has found this one of the most profound sessions – because it has quite literally changed their careers and for some it has changed their lives. It will change your focus so that you ensure your success.

Most leaders and managers of people just go about their daily routines, trying to do their best getting through their emails and their piles of 'to do's' but don't think about the greater question about 'why' they are doing 'it'. So they continue to do it exactly the same, day in day out, fighting fires and then they continue to get more and more of what they already have. Is that you?

Knowing your vision and knowing how you will get there will enable you to spend your time wisely doing only the things that will bring you success. Go back now to Part One Chapter One page 19 and revisit what you said in Be the Greatest Leader you can Be – Vision and Legacy.

Write it here again now:

- Legacy

- Vision

The first step in starting to create your vision is to map out your critical relationships. Start with the end in mind. We are going to start with one of your most critical areas – your home life. This is where your leadership is the most vital to your health and well-being and to those people around you. This is where your leadership will make a significant difference.

Personal - Key Relationships

Stop and think for a moment about the key people in your life – not just your career – and name them here. Let's start with your family and friends, the people who are really important to you. Who are they?

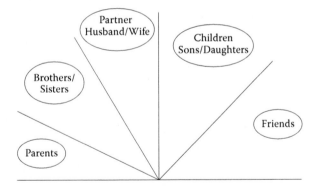

Coaching Moment

Choose one relationship you want to improve that will make the biggest difference to you personally. Benchmark the relationship, now based on how 'fulfilled' you are in this relationship – go on, be brave – it's only from this point that you can improve it and no one needs to know, do they? Now that you know where you are now, give yourself a 'challenge' to improve 'it' by end of this year.

> What is your vision of success for this relationship?
>
> What will you do to improve this relationship?
>
> What is the one question you need to ask this person that, if you knew the answer, would make the biggest difference to you?
>
> How are you making this person wrong?
>
> What is your first step?

Leadership – Key Relationships

Now do the same for your leadership role. List all the key people that you need to influence.

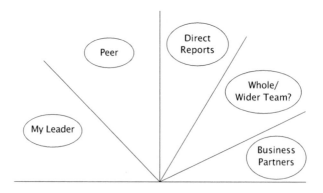

Coaching Moment

Take all the relationships listed and benchmark between 0 (low) and 10 (high).

Now put another number which will indicate where you want to be with this person in three to six months' time.

What is your vision of success?

What actions do you need to take to improve this relationship now?

What do you need to do differently to be successful?

What do you need to stop doing?

What is your first step?

Commit to keep trying.

This will provide you with a map of 'who' to influence and also where the relationship is now and where it needs to be to ensure your success. Be honest and go with your intuition. There is no wrong answer to this – it is your benchmark.

As a leader you will be leading a direct report team and a wider team. List down by name each of your direct reports, being very honest. Before any team event and/or meeting, take some time to prepare as above to ensure you maximise the time you have with those people who can make a significant difference to your results.

If you have a larger, wider team think also about them as a whole group and ask yourself the same questions as above – then take action.

Get very clear on the top three or four things that you want them to say about you. Then ask yourself honestly: where are you now and what do you have to do to ensure they say what you want them to say in years to come?

For example, from when my son was 15 until he was 19 he had 'typical' teenage issues and it was really frightening to experience. I was a single mother with no one to share the burden or anxiety of what was happening. My vision was, and is 'To be the best Mum I can be'. I used this all the way through this period of our lives. It enabled me to look ahead over the present, continually aiming for success. It enabled me to see what I needed to see and to have the conversations I needed to have to help him. I had to coach myself continuously through this period, knowing if I reacted without thinking first I would alienate him and possibly lose him. I had to remember every day what my vision was and 'act as if' which meant:

- Treat him like an adult

- Be clear on the boundaries of what was and what was not acceptable behaviour

- Be there for him no matter what he did

- Get him the professional help he needed

By keeping to that, eventually, after a long battle, he is and has been for the last 10 years an amazing human being who took his life under control, faced his demons, is now very successful and with whom I have a fantastic relationship. He said to me just the other day, "I always knew you were there for me no matter what."

That was the best thing he could have said – but there were times when I didn't think I was going to get through it and there were times I didn't think he would survive it.

So when you do these exercises, take the time; they can change your whole life – not just your relationships at work but your leadership at home with the people who mean the most to you.

Continuously review. I do it yearly now but do check in: how are you doing really and what do you need to focus on for this year?

Especially with your parents. If those relationships are not clear, if you hold deep anger, resentment or guilt then you have work to do. You have conversations to have – before it's too late (see Part Two Chapter Four – page 132 Managing Conflict).

Ask yourself now what is the one question you need to ask them that would make a difference to the relationship you have with them.

Then, how would you feel if one day you didn't get the chance to ask them that question?

I did this with my father. I needed to know the answer to one question because I could never understand why he was never really happy, always negative and critical when he had a wonderful family life. It just didn't add up.

When I was brave enough to ask the question, it all fell into place and I would understand why he had been the way he had been. He said, "I never knew my father"!!! From that moment my relationship with him began to change. I was able to forgive him for his behaviours and to challenge him more freely with his comments. We became really close and very good 'friends' as he got older, so much so that when I suddenly lost him (I didn't have the time to say goodbye) I was at peace with him. No anger, no guilt, just a natural sadness of loss.

So if you don't do anything else with this book, do this for you – and for them!

Know your Leadership Legacy

You are becoming clear on what your vision is for you personally and also as a leader in your organisation. Mine is 'To be the best I can so that I can enable others to be their best'.

Your personal journey of leadership starts now. Today is a new day, so understand where you have come from (your life line) and know what your guiding principles are (your values).

Now be very clear on what your leadership legacy and purpose is.

Coaching Moment

Just stop, close your eyes and go forward in your mind to a time in the future when you've done it, you've been successful. Look down on yourself and see what you see below – see the success you have had.

What exactly have you achieved?

How are you being described?

What are they saying about your leadership?

What's working?

What has not worked and what do you need to be aware of?

Try to be very clear and precise on what you want your leadership legacy to be – because that is what will happen, so make sure it's what you will be proud of in the future.

Values

Your leadership values are a vital part of how you operate – they are not just words, clever words you see written in 'corporate' material – they should be in your DNA – they should be visible in everything you do, everything you say, all the time, everywhere, with everyone.

In my experience, one of the most critical values for every team and in every leader is TRUST. Without trust in a relationship you have nothing. You will not have any robust conversations, you will not have any commitment nor will you focus on the right results. So without trust and being trustworthy you will never be a transforming leader. It is so easy to destroy it.

Coaching Moment

So think now how important is trust and being trustworthy to you? What will you be doing?

Evidence

What behaviours will you be doing? | What behaviours will you not be doing?

Get clear on the behaviours that you commit to do now and hold yourself accountable.

Do this exercise with every key value of yours. You will most likely have no more than five or six top values and you need to be clear on the top five or six behaviours that you will and will not do to support these values. Don't compromise because you will be measured by how you behave by everyone you meet and everyone you lead.

So now you are clear, now you know to some degree of detail who you are, what you stand for and how you will behave as a leader. You know in short your vision, purpose and values as well as the impact you want to make – your leadership personality is forming.

Now it's time to get the message clear for others so that you can communicate this with passion, with commitment and with integrity.

Your Leadership Message – Your Elevator Pitch

Bearing in mind that people will generally only remember somewhere between 7% and 15% of what you say, you must make sure that your message is very clear to your team when you meet them. An elevator pitch is what it says: imagine you have just sixty seconds to influence as you travel together in an elevator.

One wrong word or a look out of place and you will cause 'doubt' and 'a lack of trust to build' in your team's minds. So ensure you get it right – especially when they don't know you well.

Coaching Moment

Take a moment now, find a large piece of paper and note down all the key words you have elicited to now:

- Your legacy and purpose

- Your vision

- Your values and your behaviours

- Your impact message

- Your strengths

- Your beliefs

- The culture and environment you want to create in your team/organisation

Now do a mind map:

Now put into words; for example here is mine:

My vision is to be the best executive and team impact coach I can be – so that you can be very successful in your life and career.

My commitment to you is:

I will always be 100% honest with you.

I will challenge your beliefs and behaviours if they are not working for you.

I will be flexible in the way we work together, always operating with absolute integrity in everything I say and do and nothing will be shared outside of this room assuring you of 100% confidentiality.

I will continuously strive to be the most creative and innovative with interventions and ensure you have the tools to enable you to be successful.

When your message is 'ready', practise it in front of a mirror; video yourself. Get it right.

Practise, practise, practise.

The words should be 'your' words, describe 'who' you really are, what drives and motivates you and what others will see and experience from you.

This should not be 'business' speak. It is the most boring language and will certainly will not inspire or motivate your team – or anyone, actually!

Speak from the heart and that will change the minds of everyone you lead. Use sensory language to bring colour and life to your message. Use metaphors to link to well-known thoughts and feelings.

Now add to it what your vision of success is for the team/ organisation. Tell them what's important to you; give them examples; bring it alive with metaphor to motivate and inspire them.

Summary

1. Know your vision of success.

2. Know what you want your legacy to be.

3. Know your critical relationships and have them all benchmarked.

4. Know your values and know the behaviours that you will do/not do.

5. Get clear on your elevator pitch – what are your critical messages?

6. Practise your elevator pitch so much that you say it with passion.

Chapter Four

Know your Impact

It's an area that is often overlooked, disregarded and thought of as irrelevant – but in my experience you do that at your peril. Every day people see you, your team see you, they hear you and make assumptions so you need to ensure that you are sending out the right messages about yourself. Over my career I have heard so much feedback about the leaders I have coached, and sadly some I have not. Direct reports have called me before I was coaching their leader. They asked me to tell him to stop 'dyeing his hair', or her to 'stop wearing too much jewellery', or them to 'have showers and use deodorant before they come to work'. As an experienced impact coach, my list goes on and on of true experiences. People describe in detail how someone dresses, how they speak, what body language signals they give out and what behaviours they consistently do. People love to talk – and talk they will, about you. Make sure it's positive.

Transforming leaders are integral – what they say is what they do. They are consistent; they are the same whether they are with you on a one-to-one or whether they are speaking to a large audience. You know where you are with them – they have integrity. Great leaders make an impact. Impact comes from both the inside and outside of you. What you are wearing and how you are behaving give someone valuable information about you as a leader.

You make an impact now and you cannot stop it happening – so it's important to know how it happens and what it is and how to change it. 90% of people form an opinion about you in 60 seconds – they think they know your age, your education, your salary, your expertise – so what are those unconscious silent messages and decisions that people make about you – are they correct or are they completely wrong? Are they what you want people to say about you? What is your impression of yourself? Take control now, it will be worth the investment.

Your Personal Impact

When did you last watch a video or DVD of yourself presenting or in a meeting? What did you think? What would you want to change? What did you like? What do you want to keep? If you have not seen yourself at work in this situation then ask someone to film you. Many people do not want to look at themselves, but every moment of every day at work people are having to look and listen to you – it is a vital part of understanding the impact you make now and creating the future impact you want to have.

Coaching Moment

Stop for a moment and find a full-length mirror and look at yourself – go on, be brave ... this is what other people see – so when you look at yourself what do you see?

Now list down here what you like when you see yourself. Everyone has 'good' points.

-
-
-
-
-

Now what don't you like? . . .

-
-
-
-
-

Now what can you control and influence about the way you look?

Emphasise your good points always and camouflage your not-so-good points.

What are you going to do now to improve your personal appearance?

List three to five things that you can control and influence:

-

-

-

-

-

Once you know what your impact is now, you've given yourself feedback and you've seen yourself in a video, you can ask for feedback from others.

At Vi International we conduct a Personal Impact 360° survey for you. We will ask your manager/ direct reports/key stakeholders to give you feedback – then we will collate that for you, create a report and feed it back to you.

It is important to stop and think now 'what impact do you want to make in the future?' Start with 'the end in mind' and then you have a vision of what you will look like.

Coaching Moment

Design your impact

Exercise

1. Think to the future now – say in three to six months' time – in terms of your impact and gravitas, what do you want to 'look' like? (Keep to positive statements)

2. What will that do for you if you achieve it?

3. Visualise it – see what you will look like

    a. Hear it – hear the sound of your voice, hear how and what you are saying

    b. How will you be feeling?

    c. What will you be doing differently?

    d. What is your body language like?

4. Next steps – what are you going to do to achieve it?

5. Who can help you? What professional help do you need?

6. List all your actions here.

Start now and improve it by using the key areas – be seen – be heard.

In the first few seconds, people will unconsciously judge you – something like 55% on your appearance and body language, 38% on your voice and only about 7% on what you say. That's why we forget people's names when we first meet them; we have so much visual data coming into our brains – something like two million bits every second – so no wonder we forget a name. By the way, if this is you why not try this exercise next time you are introduced to someone new:

Coaching Moment – remember people's names

- Take a visual photo of them in your mind

- Keep it in full colour – photo size

- Add their name somewhere in writing on the photo

- Say their name to yourself and repeat it, then say it aloud to them

It works for me when I am running new team sessions and I have 10-20 names to remember and sometimes more than that. You will not make an impact if you continually forget people's names. It is key to leadership. I know people who have a map of their people with their names attached to the photos on their office wall.

Appearance

The quickest way to improve your impact is to take a look at your appearance. Your hairstyle, skin, clothes, shoes and accessories speak volumes. Everything that someone else can see delivers a message about you. Clothes are not who we are, but they do communicate an essence of who we are. They give clues about you.

Sadly, some people think of it as 'superficial' and not important. However, it is a part of 'human behaviour'. We search for information to see if we are 'safe' – the visual data is very powerful and can't be ignored. Have you ever had that experience? I have.

A board chief executive paid no attention to his personal appearance, did not think it was important or that anyone would measure him by how he dressed. He was wrong. I had countless calls prior to coaching him from his board but also from his leaders and from HR; how could they put him in front of the media 'looking like that'? So we worked together on his appearance, although he recognised that it was more important to others than it was for himself. He changed and was able to go on television and get great feedback.

Better to be in control of the message, better to be communicating on the outside what/who you really are than getting the message very wrong – giving out the wrong messages. We see this every day at work and all around us. The mistakes people make. Here are some examples for you from our Vi Impact Seminars we have run for the last 20 years about what people want to see and what they do not.

DOs	DON'Ts
· Look in a mirror before you leave for work and during the day.	· Wear too much perfume or aftershave.
· Shower every morning and use a deodorant.	· Wear too short trousers or skirts.
· Go to your hairdresser every six weeks minimum.	· Wear stained clothes.
· Clean your shoes weekly and keep a shoe cleaning kit with you at all times.	· Smoke (it makes you smell and your clothes).
· Have your shoes heeled	· Too much makeup.
· Replace shoes when they are old.	· Too much jewellery.
· Ensure your clothes fit well and are in good condition.	· Shirts that don't fit around the neck and the stomach or are stained under the arms!
· Wear a light *eau de toilette* or aftershave.	· Too many patterns/colours at once (tie/shirt/suit).
· Ensure your clothes are clean and regularly dry-cleaned.	· Dirty stained teeth.
· Go to the dentist regularly and the hygienist.	· Nails which are dirty, bitten or stained.
· Ladies - wear a French manicure or pale natural shade of nail varnish.	· Tattoos.
· Gents - have a regular manicure.	

Now it is time to go into your wardrobe and see if you have any of the above – be brave – be in control of your visual message.

1. Throw out <u>all</u> old clothes (give them to charity) which are out of date because if you don't you will be seen as 'out of touch' with no new ideas and not able to afford anything 'new' – how successful are you?

2. Select the clothes you look and feel great in, the ones that give you impact and say what you want to say about yourself – put those aside.

3. What about your shoes? If they are 'old' or out of fashion, need repair – invest in the best you can and ensure you have good leather shoes which are comfortable. Shoes are one of the first things someone notices.

4. Go through everything you wear and take to work including bags/briefcase/pens/laptop case/pencils – these are your tools so make sure they look great too.

A senior board executive who came into an executive coaching session wearing spectacles that were taped up with plaster to hold them together – he was chief executive of one of the largest civil engineers in the world – what did that say about their organisation?

The sales executive who came in with his grey trousers sewn up with blue cotton in his crotch area, easily seen with the way he sat – what did that say about him and his company?

The female non-executive who looked too young for her age and experience – who would take her seriously? Who would think she had the experience to do her job?

My true-life examples go on and on – over my career I have seen all sorts of terrible 'image' mistakes. So make sure someone isn't laughing and talking about your impact behind your back.

Take action NOW and if you don't know what suits you have a session with an experienced impact coach. A good experienced image or impact coach will:

- Help you define what message you want to communicate

- Provide you with a colour analysis which analyses what colours suit you best and convey the right psychological message

- Do a style analysis to define what styles suit you best and communicate what you want to say

- Do a wardrobe assessment so that you only have in it what suits you and what is current and what will say what you want to say

- Give advice on all accessories

- Give you advice on hairstyle, colour and shape

- Give advice on makeup

- Give advice on skincare

Coaching Moment

Be honest with yourself right now or ask someone you trust 100% to give you feedback.

1. What are your positive attributes?

2. What are the things you need to camouflage?

3. What impact do you want to make as a leader?

4. Memorise people's names – practise

5. Improve your personal impact – do a wardrobe 'sort'

Body Language – your body language is imperative to impact and influence. You will have experienced someone with very negative posture, expressions, eye contact or gesture and will have felt what it feels like to be on the receiving end of that. With our global communities we are also experiencing many different cultures and therefore different body language signals to support the cultures. This book is not an in-depth study of body language but it is to bring you into awareness of yours and others' so that you can influence and lead successfully. Sometimes we are not aware of what we are doing, which is why feedback is so vital. Seeing yourself in action can provide you with important information as will an Executive Coaching Impact Workshop where you will be given feedback.

Quick tips for improving your body language are as follows:

Posture – Walk tall; keep your back straight even when you are seated. Walk with only your legs, not swaying your whole body from side to side!!! Watch yourself walk and pull yourself up straight. Ladies, please keep your legs together! Gents, please take your hands off the back of your heads when you are speaking or in meetings.

Expression – Smile – it costs nothing but means everything. Keep your face relaxed. Pretend you are chewing a toffee to relax the muscles, especially before 'tense', challenging situations. Stop scowling and frowning. Appear calm, interested and alert.

Eye Contact – Keep it positive. Look at where someone else is looking and mirror back what you see. I remember a sales meeting with a very senior head of UK sales for a huge organisation looking mainly at the floor whilst occasionally looking at me. I wasn't threatened and just looked at the floor with him to connect with him. Don't stare someone out. There are many different eye contact signals – just go with what you are given. By the way, it worked and I continued to support him to turn his organisation around. Different cultures have different needs and beliefs around eye contact so be aware.

Hand Movements – It is OK to be creative with your hand gestures but be aware that some people hardly use their hands. Ensure your words and your gestures match and are aligned because that is when people will truly remember what you are saying.

Space – This is a critical area in body language to ensure you don't make mistakes. Culturally it will make or break a meeting and relationship. Ensure you are always no closer than arm distance apart. When we do this on seminars it is amazing to see the differences in needs. When we ask the group to split into two lines opposite one another and then ask one group to move forward until the space is perfect for them, you can see the discomfort on the other group's faces. Some people need a lot of distance between them and another person; some people want to be a lot closer – so be careful – 'arms distance' is safe in our corporate world today.

Build Rapport by pacing someone else's body language. This takes practice and skill but it is possible if you look and take in the information you are unconsciously being given and act on it, mirroring back what you are experiencing – but please be subtle and no copying; it's incongruent and you will fail. The worst mistake I made early in my career was not to pick up on the body language I was seeing at a sales meeting. He was low energy, little movement, straight-on eye contact and no hand signals. I was high energy, flexing eye contact and very creative hand signals. So we were totally mismatched. Needless to say, I did not get a second meeting or the contract. The lesson was a powerful one for me. Remember, sometimes you are not told exactly why you have not been successful just 'we found someone who fitted our needs more closely' or 'we are reconsidering and will be in touch at a later date'. You will never be told it was your body language or your appearance. So be aware that your body language signals can put people off, can alienate you and can send the wrong message about you. Look at the other person's energy: is it high, medium or low and mirror back what you are experiencing. Practise now.

Coaching Moment

Body language

Try and take video of yourself at a meeting or a presentation so that you can see what you do. Reflect back on any feedback you have had over the years. Look in a mirror and video yourself again.

- Stand tall. Hold yourself straight from the tips of your toes to the top of your head. Walk with your legs, not your whole body

- When sitting, sit with a straight back. Avoid curving the spine

- Relax your shoulders and your body of any tension

- Be aware of the expression on your face – smile and acknowledge people as you walk around. Connect with them

- Keep eye contact and look positive

- Be aware of how you use your hand gestures

- Mirror back what other people are 'giving' you in terms of energy

Be heard – your voice is one of your most important tools for making an impact and communicating your message. It's your responsibility to be heard and yet most people don't like the sound of their voice. Great leaders make powerful speakers. People want to listen to them and they are remembered for what they say.

We all remember people who have tremendous voices who we could listen to all day, the ones we want to listen to, we hang on to their every word and we remember what they said. Conversely, we also can remember people who switched us off.

Think now of that someone whose voice you admire and why? What qualities were/are present?

- Name:

- Qualities:

We can all also think of people who we couldn't hear, we couldn't understand, who were boring and monotonous – who we just wanted to stop talking.

Coaching Moment

Exercise

Think of that person now. What was it that you didn't like?

- Name:

- Qualities:

The only way you will know what your voice is like is if you record yourself speaking normally, not in a presentation. If you are to develop your impact, influence and leadership, your voice is critical.

Now take some time to record yourself – just talk about a hobby or something you are working on. Take the time – let yourself talk for a few minutes. Replay it.

Then do this exercise:

What do you hear?

What strikes you?

What do you like about your voice?

What don't you like?

Then reflect on any feedback that you've had.

There are key areas you can start developing now that, if you practise daily, will improve the quality of your voice:

Volume – loud enough to be heard.

Speed – fast enough to be clear but not too slow so that people switch off.

Intonation – interesting pitch and fall so that you keep people interested and connected to you and your message.

Pause – enough to add impact so they remember what you have said.

They are all controlled by your breathing. It is important to develop your breathing techniques in order to have impact with your voice. It may be wise to hire a voice coach to develop yours but there are some simple techniques you can practise with. It's a bit like going to the gym because you do have to practise to get the muscles strengthened.

So try this exercise now but, be warned, you do need to find a place which is quiet.

Coaching Moment

Stand up – feet hip-distance apart, with a straight spine, neck and chin up, looking straight ahead. Legs slightly bent at the knees. Keep your arms by your side. Now practise reading a poem, a newspaper, a presentation or your elevator pitch.

Record it.

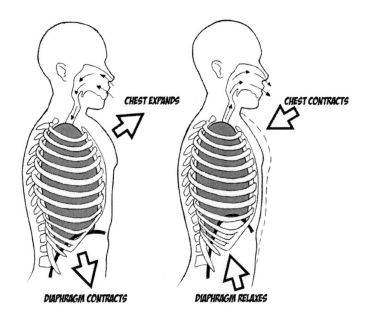

Notice

- Where are you breathing from? High (throat) Middle (mid-chest) Low (diaphragm)?

- Put the flat of your hand on the area just above your navel – that is your lower diaphragm

- Breathe down to there

- Breathe in for a count of eight

- Breathe out for a count of eight

Now

- Put words to it

- Practise again

- Speaking on the outward breath

Continue to breathe deeply

- Use the vowel sounds

- Use the consonants

- Use your breath to accentuate your words

- Find your 'best' number of words per intake of air – so that you are clear

- Stop at the end of each sentence – pause

- Posture – stand or sit with as straight a back as possible

Now record again and hear the difference. Just with a little practice and awareness you can develop your voice.

So what are you going to do to improve your voice?

-

-

-

Do you need a voice coach?

It will be worth it if you need to do a lot of public speaking.

So now you are more aware of your impact and how to improve it using the vital areas of:

Appearance

Body language

Voice

A transformational leader will pay attention and develop all these areas and you can learn to do this easily. We are not taught at school or university and sometimes our parents do not have the skills to train us. So it is no wonder so many get it wrong. There are highly-experienced and trained professionals to help you.

Make sure if you are in the corporate world that you choose someone who has relevant corporate experience and knowledge – then you know you will be getting the best training for your business goals.

Communicate who you are with your personal impact and that will ensure people receive the 'right' message about you even before they have got to know you.

Now you are ready to bring the team together and design your journey of developing a high-performing and successful team.

Summary

1. Create your leadership impact message.

2. Improve your personal appearance.

3. Improve your body language.

4. Improve your vocal delivery.

5. Video yourself and record yourself.

6. Work on what you can control and influence.

7. Continually review to stay current.

8. Find professional help if you cannot help yourself.

PART TWO
Transform Your Team

Chapter One

Get to know them

So now you are ready to start the process of building a winning team, a team that works well together and achieves the greatest of results, better than any other team in your organisation, better than your competitors.

In my experience, great teams:

- Know one another

- Know their leader

- Understand their similarities

- Accept their differences

- Know their combined strengths

- Support each other

- Have a shared vision, values and purpose

- Have robust and courageous conversations

- Share issues and challenges together

- Have strong, successful stakeholder relationships

- Focus on success

- Have fun

Team Coaching Moment

Where are you?

Stage 1	Stage 2	Stage 3	Stage 4
· New team · Any tension? · Any caution? · Polite and nice? · Quiet? · Surface level dscussions? · People do not know one another? · Optimism?	· Difficulties and concerns being raised? · Frustrations visible? · Relationship problems? · Silos - focus on own results? · Arguments? · Targets not achieved?	· Debate starting? · Constructive challenge? · Getting to know one another? · Trust building? · Relationships building? · Successful results starting? · Support being offered?	· Taking personal accountability? · Holding one another accountable? · Having great courageous conversations? · Supporting one another? · Successful results? · Great leadership?

Get to know your team

Whatever stage you are at, one of the most vital areas for you to consider is to get to know and understand your team and its members. You are ready for this step now, having prepared yourself in Part One. Don't try to skip that part, in my experience it will not work. You will only be a great leader if you work on yourself first and you probably know that deep inside yourself. If you have ever failed to build a successful team or if you are new to leading a team, it is even more important that you start with yourself.

Take the time to get to know them – really understand them. Spend time with them, both on a one-to-one basis and in team meetings, and take time out together. Why not book all one-to-ones in your calendar now for the year ahead?

Your team are not mind readers – they don't know how much you care or are genuinely interested in them until you show them.

In other words, demonstrate clearly and regularly to your team that they are important to you by giving them your time.

So it is up to you. Evidence proves that a leader who spends time with his/her team, and leads with integrity, establishes a high level of trust, encourages open and honest debate and will gain loyalty and commitment from his/her team that will lead to achieving greater results together.

Advice I received from a successful leader after I worked with his team is to recruit for diversity, not in your own image. That way, you fill the gaps, have different strengths and will therefore make better, more informed decisions and achieve success much more quickly. For sure, you need the right team around you, the team that has the skills to be successful – and those skills will be different.

High-performing teams don't just happen – they are skilfully built by great leaders. There is an informal climate, where people are encouraged to say what they think, where there is little 'second guessing' and where people are willing to take risks and learn from their mistakes. Team members will support their colleagues. There are no failures, only feedback, and problems are seen as a solution to find. Team members know one another and can tap into their different strengths and personality differences. There is no discounting of others. People are free to be themselves and acknowledge others for their differences. Time is not wasted, decisions are made quickly and the team pulls together for success.

Bring your team together and ask them the following questions at your next meeting.

Team Coaching Moment

Think about a great team that you have been in – what was it like? What was present and evident?

- .

- .

- .

What was the effect on you being in this team?

Now consciously think about one of the most difficult teams you have been in and what was present.

- .

- .

What was the effect on you?

So if you don't put in the time and the effort, guess which team you will be leading?

Step 1 – One-to-ones – take to next stage

Ensure you have regular one-to-ones with each of your team. Mistakes leaders make is to keep these one-to-ones just for reviewing the 'action' and 'to do' lists and not spending any time on the things that really matter to the team member or leader. This will build a deep sense of frustration and resentment with your team members and you will not know what's really going on. Trust will not build and a climate of fear could emerge.

Take an hour, go off site and take time getting to know them and understand them and let them get to know you. That time will be repaid over and over again. Remember, the more 'difficult' a team member, the longer you need to spend with them and the deeper and more honest the discussion you need to have.

Ensure every team member has a Personal Development Plan every year and mentor and coach them to success.

Don't wait and hope that the team will build. It won't; it will function, but not successfully, and you are likely to find that the team will work in silos with high levels of fear and a lack of trust will form. People will become defensive and cover up mistakes and the team will not achieve targets.

Step 2 – Regular team meetings

Organise regular team meetings and some team-building events throughout the year. Ensure also that there is some time for socialising so that people find more personal connections and deepen their relationships.

Team Coaching Moment

Start with understanding the current team climate. You may decide to ask someone in the organisation, or a team facilitation coach, to conduct some confidential interviews with each of your team so that you are all aware and you have an independent view.

Otherwise, you can do this yourselves; take the time to record the information on flip charts and ensure this is all recorded and goes out to every team member following your meeting:

- What is working well now and we want to keep?

- What is not working and we need to change?

- What strengths do we have – what are we very good at?

- What is the level of trust in the team now and what needs to change?

- How well do the team know one another and their roles, responsibilities and backgrounds?

- What is the level of support in the team – how supported do you feel?

Remember, some people may come into these events feeling unsure and anxious. They may have had previous experiences which were difficult or they may actually dislike or distrust one another. So remember – it will take time, patience and determination, but let nothing stop you from building your team.

I remember back to an event when two people walked in and proceeded to avoid each other most of the day. I knew there was some negative history between them and the effect of their behaviour was a concern. The effect inside of themselves must have been very uncomfortable and the effect on the team would have been very detrimental had it continued. Now they needed to work together in this team. With the executive coaching which was part of the event, they were able to put the past behind them, have a discussion and become very good colleagues and now friends – they are still in contact now even though they work in different organisations. I saw them transform their relationship and it transformed the team – they did it. They were brave and they had the right conversation (the one that should have happened years before). The difference was awesome to see.

Step 3 – Understand the differences

Take some time on the first event to build an understanding of the different personality types. You could use a well-known psychometric like the Myers Briggs Type Indicator (MBTI*).

Step 4 – Share career timelines

Share your 'life lines' – as you prepared in Part One (Chapter One page 24). Ask the team to come prepared to share the highs and lows of their career and what they have learned from them.

---

* MBTI is a trademark or registered trademark of the Myers-Briggs Type Indicator Trust in the United States and other countries

Team Coaching Moment

You have all been asked to prepare your career timeline – please share those with us now, highlighting the highs and the lows and what you learned from them.

Each person to take the time to share and then ask the question "What did you learn about your colleagues and how can this help you to build a great team?"

Be aware that in some cultures alcohol is acceptable; also be aware that in some it is totally unacceptable. Words and actions cannot be undone. Words cannot be unsaid. So avoid anything that could cause issues.

I remember a team I heard about who did exactly that and, as a result, trust was destroyed that evening. Things were said that were regretted – but they could not be unsaid. The team eventually lost its leader and several members left; people were left very under-resourced.

Step 5 – Establish current reality

Bring the team together for half a day and take time to establish the current reality. If you have many issues and know you have a dysfunctional team, you will probably need to hire in an external professional facilitator.

Team Coaching Moment

- What are we doing well and why?

- What successes as a team have we had in the last three to six months?

- What are we not doing well – what are our gaps?

- What are the top three big issues – what are the top three challenges?

- What does the team need to do to be successful?

It is vitally important to take the time to understand these areas and talk them all through. Ensure everyone contributes – allow the time to talk. Don't lead them – let them lead themselves.

Step 6 – Ask the right questions

At each and every event, think of a few interesting and fun questions to pose that will allow people to get to know one another better.

People like talking about themselves and they like hearing about who they are working with. The more people know about each other, the greater the trust will be. So be brave, be courageous and ask the questions.

Team Coaching Moment
Getting to know you even better.

Ask two or three of these questions at each team meeting to find out more about one another:

- Three reasons why I would enjoy working with me:

- Three reasons why I would find it difficult to work with me:

- If I were not here right now I would be...

- A phrase I use too often is...

- I wish I did not...

- I am not good at...

- My ideal night out is...

- In weak moments I...

- If I wasn't doing this job I would be...

- In a nutshell my philosophy on life is...

- What inspired you to embark on this career?

- When you were 15 what did you want to be?

- What is the proudest moment of your working life?

- What is your most embarrassing moment?

- Whom do you most admire and why?

- Who has had the biggest influence on you?

- What career ambition do you want to achieve before you retire?

- What event altered the course of your career?

Step 7 – Gain commitment

Prepare an action plan to transform your team together.

Team Coaching Moment
Transform your team

What exactly do you all need to do in the next:

- · 90 days? What has to have been achieved? Start with the end in mind

- · 60 days? What is our halfway stage to success?

- · 30 days? What do we need to do now?

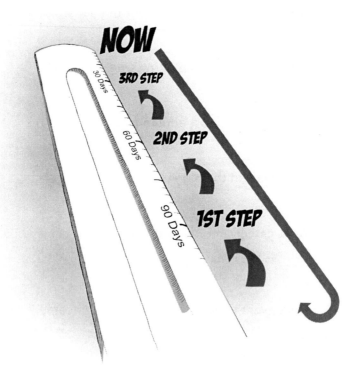

What will we do differently?

So take the time – and take more time if your team is underperforming or is new, take even more time if you have significant issues in your business.

I was brought in to work with a very senior global board that was underperforming, with deep mistrust between individuals and the new leader. The team was not achieving its targets and, as a result, there was a deep feeling of fear. The individuals were operating in silos and small teams and alienating the leader. At the first two-day event we created a safe 'environment' for sharing, understanding the current reality and being honest about what worked and what didn't. They shared career timelines, personality differences and ways of working with conflict. The leader and the individuals were at times uncomfortable, trying to divert back to the 'business' issues; big egos were at play, but they stuck with it – even the leader. It was a very tough journey but they did it. They took the time, they started working better together, they got to know each other on a much deeper level. By knowing and understanding one another, the barriers came down. Individuals' confidence levels grew. The negative behaviours changed and, in their place, absolute integrity was evident. The team played to their strengths and understood and worked with their differences.

So even with the most dysfunctional of teams, you can transform them together.

Summary

1. Get to know your team individually and together.

2. Book your one-to-ones and team meetings for the year ahead.

3. Elicit the team climate.

4. Use psychometrics to understand one another and your differences.

5. Share your career time lines.

6. Establish the current reality of the team.

7. Get to know one another.

8. Gain commitment – prepare a 90/60/30-day action plan.

Chapter Two

Build the Trust

Trust, I have found, is the most important and vital of all the values in any relationship and in every team. It's the most critical of all the steps to building a high-performing team – or any relationship. You have completed this exercise earlier in this guide so use this at a team meeting to establish what is important for the team (Part One Chapter Three, page 56).

Team Coaching Moment

What is important to you about trust in this team? What will we be doing and what will we not be doing?

What behaviours will we adhere to?

.

.

.

.

List the top five behaviours you will see, hear and experience in this team.

What will we now commit not to do?

.

The most important aspect to building trust is time – so invest in it. At every meeting be determined to get to know one another on a deeper level.

Trust is never complete and it is a continuous journey. You can never 'assume' it's there or 'hope' it's there. You have to work at it and if it's not there, you need to know and take action.

The biggest reason I have discovered in my experience why people don't trust each other is often because they don't know or understand one another. They don't know who they really are, what motivates them, what their fears are, what their strengths are. This creates misunderstanding and the potential for disagreements.

Another reason is that they can have had a negative experience with each other at an earlier time which has caused the trust to break. Past experiences, if not resolved, will impact every relationship and lead to the team's failure.

It may need a clear, open discussion (see Have the Right Conversation Part Two Chapter Four page 137) and may need expert facilitation and/or one-to-one coaching.

A few years ago we had to be involved in some 'expert three-way' facilitation between a chief executive and a chairman that was amazing. Two Alpha Males with huge egos, two huge brains, two amazing individuals with huge strengths BUT whose relationship had broken down over a series of issues over the years. It had got to the point where there was no trust, they did not talk unless they had to and not about anything that they should discuss, so they ignored the 'elephants in the room', they were not aligned and this was showing itself in board meetings in front of key stakeholders as they blamed one another – like open warfare. It was incredibly tense and team members were ill at ease, waiting for the outburst of temper. Anxiety and fear were evident at every meeting. We held in-depth confidential interviews with each person to understand what had happened, then each person had individual coaching. Only when they were ready we brought them together to facilitate the in-depth discussions they needed and to agree the way forward of how they would work together. It took only two three-way meetings. They resolved their differences and went on to have very good professional success together, and so did the board!

So if they can do it – so can you.

Trust will build if the team are:

- Open and honest

- Brave and courageous – say what needs to be said

- Consistent with their behaviour – don't say one thing and then do something different

- Interested in others – listen to one another and be prepared to listen to feedback and change behaviours

- Open about their strengths and weaknesses – be vulnerable and share them

- Prepared to take responsibility – you are responsible for your behaviours

At each event/meeting ensure that trust is a key focus and remember never to assume it's there.

Steps to building trust are:

Step One – Continue getting to know one another on a personal level. The more you know and understand one another, the deeper the trust will be.

Step Two – Start sharing 'who' you are. Ask everyone to share.

Team Coaching Moment

Exercise – in a team.

The top three strengths I bring to this team are:

You can trust me to always:

What motivates me in a team is:

What demotivates me is:

Give everyone time to prepare for this session, and when in the session ensure that you allow everyone time to complete – don't rush this exercise.

- Do listen carefully (nothing else going on)

- Do watch their body language and your own

- Do say thank you

- Do take the time (five minutes each x eight directors and yourself = 45 minutes)

Step 3 – Check in - As with every team exercise you will need to do this afterwards, as follows:

Team Coaching Moment

So what did you learn?

What difference will that make to the team?

What will you do differently knowing this information?

If you are listening and watching intently, you will see people connecting, people understanding, people relaxing with one another. The energy in the room will change – it will feel much more positive.

Step 4 – Share yourself

As the leader of this team it's important for you to show the lead; lead from the front, be brave and be open. So if the team are hesitant, go first. Establish yourself, show your vulnerabilities – go on, you can do it. You will be surprised at what a huge difference this can make.

You may be taking over an existing team, you may be replacing a 'great' leader, you may be leading your peers. This is still a vital step. You cannot assume they trust you as their leader – you need to establish yourself.

Start by sharing:

- Your career life line

- Your personality traits, strengths and gaps

- Your motivations and drivers

- Your mistakes and the learning you had

- What support you need for them

- What you want to keep in the team and what you want to change

Put your mark on the team, it's your team. Establish yourself, the past is the past – it's NOW.

Establish rapport with each member of your team and connect with them.

Step 5 – Team share the same as above for the leader

Now the individuals share exactly the same as the leader.

Once completed, now ask yourselves:

What did we learn from this exercise and what difference will it make to the level of trust in our team?

Step 6 – Build Rapport

The team need to build a rapport with one another. There are three key areas to building rapport in any culture. Sometimes leaders only concentrate on their content and forget about 'how' they are communicating. Remember the chapter on Impact and Building Rapport. (Part One Chapter Four page 74)

The meaning of the communication is the effect it has on the recipient. Communication is much more than the words we use; it is how we present ourselves to the world using our physiology and tonality of our voice as well as the language we use. Global teams and teams with cross-cultural members need to be very aware of the body language they are using.

Match the other person's
ENERGY LEVEL

Match or mirror the other person's
RHYTHM
e.g. Voice
Body Language
Posture
Breathing

...PACE...

Continue to subtly
MATCH/MIRROR
e.g. Voice
Body Language
Posture
Breathing

...PACE...

You have now established
RAPPORT

...LEAD...
to achieve your outcome

Team Coaching Moment
Build rapport using body language

The team needs to sit in two rows opposite one another. Decide which row is Team A and which is Team B.

Exercise 1

Team A – Talk about something you are passionate about

Team B – Agree verbally and copy exactly every movement and gesture

Exercise 2

Team A – Continue talking about your topic

Team B – Disagree verbally but mirror the body language signals

Exercise 3

Team A – Continue talking as above

Team B – Agree verbally but mismatch totally every body language signal

Repeat with Team B doing the talking so that everyone has the experience.

Check in with the learning:

What did you learn from this exercise?

As a team what do we need to be aware of?

This simple and fun exercise will demonstrate to the team the importance of experiencing and 'pacing' other people's body language signals to ensure that communication is not misunderstood.

I remember working with a global sales team and this exercise was fascinating and fun to do with them. We knew the people who were not working well together so we partnered them up. They all had very different cultures and therefore body language needs. It brought into their awareness the different needs and how vital it was to recognise another person's 'map of the world'.

The meaning of your communication is the response it elicits from the recipient. Communication is much more than just the words we use; it is how we present ourselves to the world using our physiology and tonality as well as the language we use.

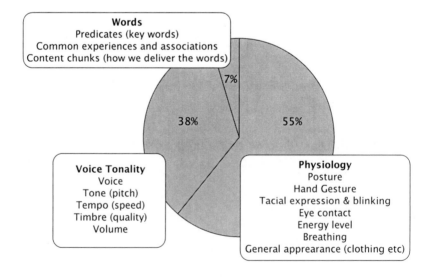

Over the last 25 years, I have experienced the most horrendous *faux pas* by senior leaders. Imagine this example: during a discussion designed to build trust, a huge new team of 25 global leaders came together in one large conference room; all different – different cultures, languages, genders!!! You can imagine how vital this event was. So put yourself in my shoes; I can see the leader 'nodding off' – yes, going to sleep. He kept trying to wake himself up – Help! So I stopped the session and asked everyone to take a break of 15 minutes. I took him aside at break time to find out what was going on and to give him feedback. It was tough for him as he was seriously jet-lagged. He had just flown in from the US that morning but the team did not know this and he was also dealing with some huge dispute with his board CFO. So we agreed that he would share with the team why he was so tired, that he was not bored and that he was dealing with a serious issue, which meant that he may have to take time out. As an introverted leader he had not thought to be upfront with them.

- When people are speaking, please remember to always:

- Look at them and connect with them

- Nod your head in agreement if you are agreeing

- Only listen to them, not your 'inner voice'

- Turn towards them as if they are the only person in the room

- Thank them

Don't be the leader who, while a direct report was sharing, was checking his Blackberry, totally discounting him, and another who carried on using his PC.

Be the leader who listens and remembers what that person has said.

Step 7 – Use psychometrics to understand

The team can use some professional psychometrics to help the building of trust. Those with a good track-record of validity and reliability, and those that are used and known by a great number of people, are the best because you can trust them.

You will probably need an expert facilitator to administer these; you may have access to an expert in your organisation's HR department. If not, you will find a list of contacts at the end of the guide, or just contact us www.viinternational.com.

By using these psychometrics, you can fast-track building the trust and respect in your team. The psychometrics I have used which I can highly recommend are:

Myers Briggs Type Indicator (MBTI* Step 1 and/or Step 2)

By knowing and understanding the MBTI* of yourself and your team, the team will:

- Improve communication by learning how different personalities communicate and be able to influence them

- Improve decision-making by understanding how the different types make decisions

- Improve time management by understanding what motivates and demotivates different personality types

* MBTI is a trademark or registered trademark of the Myers-Briggs Type Indicator Trust in the United States and other countries

- Know and understand the strengths of the team

- Be able to assess the 'blind spots' or gaps in the team

- Improve 'stress' management by understanding the 'stressors and energisers' of each team member

- Improve the perception of the team to its stakeholders

I remember a time with a team who had a leader who was 'Introverted'. They were frustrated and irritated by her because she often arrived and went straight into her office without saying 'good morning', stayed in her office with the door closed most of the day and sat on her own at lunch – then went home after her team had gone home. There were no team events and meetings were not spent sharing and discussing critical issues. They often found things out after they had happened and were not included in decisions.

The MBTI* highlighted the differences between the Extroversion and Introversion personalities, alerted the E's to their behaviours and gave the I's tools to push back and be heard. The session enabled the team to give feedback to their leader in a 'safe' environment. It also highlighted why the team was not visionary and did not want to stay in the present and sort out the issues, whilst the leader was very detailed and wanted everything discussed in infinite detail. The team also did not have high Employee Engagement scores; in fact they were terrible. The MBTI* highlighted why this could be and they were able to put in place some critical actions to ensure their focus was on the employee as well as the financials. The 'leader' was able to understand the impact of her behaviour and also the team to understand what their leader needed to work effectively. They, as a team, were also alerted to their 'blind spots' so they could cover them.

---

* MBTI is a trademark or registered trademark of the Myers-Briggs Type Indicator Trust in the United States and other countries

A facilitated MBTI* session will take a minimum of four hours if done professionally, with each person taking the questionnaire prior to the event, having some one-to-one feedback in advance. Then at the session:

Team Coaching Moment

Everyone to share their results on a team chart. Map the different profiles.

Highlight the leader's profile. What impact could this have? Discuss and agree:

- Strengths of the team – what skills does this give the team?

- Blind spots – what should the team 'be aware of'?

- How can the team improve communication?

- How can the team improve decision-making?

- How can the team improve time management?

- How can the team improve team meetings?

- How can the team improve its results?

The upfront investment financially and in time will achieve a huge return on investment for you and the team and give life skills which you will all remember – and can help you achieve harmony at home!

Step 8 - Socialise and have fun

Many leaders fail because they don't pay any attention to going out with their team and having fun. Try it and see what benefits it can bring – you will be very surprised.

'Fun and enjoyment' is one of our critical needs and values. People who enjoy coming to work, who enjoy working together, who have shared 'fun' moments together find that they can work better together when the tough times happen – and those times will happen in any team in any business. Invest now and you will see the dividends later. It is like putting deposits in your bank account ready for when you need them.

So what can you do easily? Why not ask the team what they would like to do? Teams that I know have come up with some great ideas, for example:

- Go to the theatre or have dinner

- Go to the circus or paint-balling or go-karting

- Learn how to cook together

- Help a charity for a day – give something back

- Go bowling

- Learn to sail

- Get fit – go cycling, go for a charity walk or run!!!

Be inventive and be creative, and remember it doesn't have to cost a lot!

Whatever you do, make sure it's fun, enjoyable and sometimes nothing to do with 'work'.

You will create a great energy in your team and create memorable events that people talk about forever.

Just the other day I was checking in with a leader who I had worked with three years ago. He had just come back from a leaving party with a team he used to lead and he told me, "The conversation kept coming back to the memorable team-building sessions we had and, without prompting, they remembered the sessions many years earlier for building trust in our team. Nicola brought in a prison officer who showed us how a team need to really trust one another in the most extreme of circumstances. The fact they were still talking about it said a lot to me about the lasting impact of this work."

So if you take the time with your team and create some interesting interventions, you too can be remembered years afterwards.

Take the time to have 'fun' – build the rapport and the trust and then you can achieve great business results.

Summary – Building trust

1. Take the time.

2. Value of trust – what behaviours are important for the team?

3. Continue getting to know one another.

4. Share yourself as a leader – career life line.

5. Each team member shares about themselves – career life line.

6. Build rapport.

7. Use psychometrics to understand the similarities and differences.

8. Socialise and have fun!

Chapter Three

Create a Shared Vision and Values

It is the glue that holds a team together through periods of great change and uncertainty and it is the difference that makes the difference between teams that are high-performing and those that are not!

A leader who works with his team to create a shared vision will lead, motivate and inspire loyalty, commitment and focus. It becomes the spirit of the team. It helps guide the team to make the right decisions and enable shared success.

Vision is probably the most over-used and least understood word around in our corporate world today – but it is the one thing that, once discovered, will lead a team and organisation to ultimate success. It will ensure a leader is remembered for many, many years after they have left and perhaps throughout the careers of their employees.

Take my own business – we have been through three recessions and we have survived them. Why? It is because of 'who we are' and 'how we do' what we do and the results we achieve for our clients. Our vision as a team is 'To be the Most Trusted Supplier to our Global Clients of Executive and Team Coaching'. This has meant that, over the years, our focus has always been on the client and delegates to ensure we deliver the most successful dynamic results.

A clear identity and vision will unite you; it will pull you together, focus your mind and guide you through the tough times. It will also ensure you keep attracting new talent to your organisation and it will ensure you achieve your targets.

It is the brand of the team – it will inspire and guide and ensure your team stands out from the rest. It will transform the team.

Team Coaching Moment

The Leader – share your vision

The first step to creating a shared vision with your team is for you to share your vision of success. Remember you did this in Part One – Chapter Three page 48. So when you bring your team together for a 'visioning' day, the first part of the day is to spend maybe 15-20 minutes just talking (not as a Powerpoint presentation please!) from the heart about how you see the team in, say, a year's time when it is high-performing.

I remember when a CEO of a huge corporate did this with her team. She had never talked to them about her vision in this way before; the result was amazing and they were mesmerised. The team were on the way to high performing but not there yet – something was missing. The team were in awe of her, concerned about her direct approach. They all imagined she wanted something different and was motivated by different values. They were too siloed in their approach and too present-focused. This was the piece that made the difference. They did not challenge their leader but, once they knew she wanted the challenge, they were free to do that. They still talk about it now and have all moved on to different roles in different organisations and all have used his process with their own teams.

Don't hold back. Just tell them from the heart, use metaphors, give examples of what it will be like when this team is high-performing. What will be present? Start with what is important for you, what you want to see, feel and hear. Words change minds so remember to use simple words and inject some emotion and passion into your voice and body language. Make it meaningful so you build a connection and, above all, take the time – don't rush it. It will make a huge difference for you to share what you want to see.

Team Coaching Moment

Team share their vision

What is your vision for this team? This is a shared experience so have two or three flip charts around the room and split the team into two or three groups, depending on numbers. You want about three or four in a group and you will need about 45 minutes.

Exercise

When this team is high-performing and successful what will be present?

The leader can step back now.

(Take yourself out of the room and give them time alone)

If the team want you to stay, stay and be part of the exercise – but let them ask you!

Team Coaching Moment

List on the flip charts everything that will be there and be present in this team when it is successful.

What do you want to see, feel and hear?

What are your expectations?

There are no wrong answers – just say what you think – it's OK. Every thought is important so write it down.

When we did this with another senior team who did not know or trust their new leader, the exercise was very successful. The team worked together and he worked on his own in a different room doing the same exercise – so he did not share first. Then they came back together and he went first and shared from the heart what he wanted for the team. As he was sharing his ideas, the team were hearing that there were huge similarities in what they had on their flip charts. I could see the surprise on their faces as they heard him. They then shared their thoughts with him and he had the same reaction. It was an incredible experience to see the rest of the team and the leader uniting at that moment, making it much easier to talk about what their issues were later. This was a pivotal event in building this team.

Remember this when you all come back into the room to share the flip charts – there will probably be many similar ideas and common themes which will make it easier.

Team Coaching Moment

Take the time to listen, absorb and to really hear what the team are saying – don't discount anything anyone has said – it is all valid. Everyone must be a part of this discussion. Encourage everyone to take part and voice their opinions.

This is a good time to have lunch or at least a 30 minute break to stop and reflect, because it's a defining moment in the team's journey and will be meaningful to every team member.

When you come back, bring out on a separate flip chart all the common themes and similar ideas – get clear on what will be present as a team.

Remember, it is the spirit of the team, and on the flip charts will most likely be the team's:

- Core values and operating principles

- Core purpose

- Beliefs

- Leadership behaviours

- The future culture

So it's worth it to take the time to capture the essence and be relentless, honest and totally committed to achieving it. These are very important aspects to building a successful team.

It is what you all want, need and expect for success and it will be different for every team.

This process should take up to an hour, but if it takes longer then let that happen. Creating your identity as a team is vital, so don't watch the clock.

Teams that have enduring success know their:

· Purpose

· Vision of success

· Values and operating principles

· Beliefs that drive success

· Behaviours that ensure success

· Environment and culture that will create success

So right now you have consolidated the flip charts into one or two sheets with some clear definitions of what 'this' team will be like when it's successful and now it's time to think about its core purpose.

Core Purpose – is the reason this team is in existence – it is the 'why are you here' question – it is your identity – it's a reason to be not an action list!

Team Coaching Moment

Exercise – ask the team these questions:

> Why are we here? Why does our team exist?

> Why else?

Pull all the information out on flip charts and keep going until you achieve a clear statement.

And then:

> Question: What would our key internal stakeholders say about why we are here?

And then:

> Question: What would our customers say about why we are here?

> Question: What would our wider team say about why we are here?

The reason you think you are here and what your stakeholders/ customers or wider team think may be two entirely different things, so it is vital to ensure alignment.

Continue with another even deeper question if you are not getting to a clearly-defined purpose.

> What would be lost if we didn't exist?

Your team's purpose should guide and inspire you.

Our purpose is 'To Enable You To Be Your Best'

Your purpose should be defined in no more than six to nine words – less is more and will motivate and inspire your team; it should last forever and never be 100% achievable.

Values

Be clear on your team's core values. Values are not just 'words' picked out of a management book – they are the guiding principles which define how you will operate, lead, motivate and inspire everyone you need to influence.

Team Coaching Moment

Exercise – go back to Exercise 1 (Part Two - Chapter Two – Build the Trust exercise – page 99) You know the one most critical value needed to build a high-performing team is the value of trust. Now it is time to elicit all the team's values. Look back at the flip charts that the team created about what your team will be like, and identify some key values.

Example: a CEO asked everyone to put on post-its their own values and what was important to them. This worked well and we had about 20 values and beliefs and behaviours. Values are one or two word statements, for example: trust, respect, honesty, integrity, freedom etc. They cannot be put into a container like money, a great bonus or a trip to Vegas. They are not sentences – they are simple words but they mean everything.

The team's values need to incorporate every team member's personal values – it is what the individuals bring to work every day – it's who they are. Values are what they would tell their children about what is important as they guide them in life. Be aware though, values rarely change once embedded so you cannot tell someone what values are important to them. That is why this is such an important step for a team because it is the bringing together of everyone's core operating principles. It is the way they live their lives.

Team Coaching Moment

In order to elicit a team's values it's vital to be relentless and to allow for total honesty.

There should be no more than five or six and they should be positive, meaningful and inspirational.

Exercise – depending on the size of the team, split into two or three groups of three or four and pair up to find out:

What values are important to you in a team? What do you have to have present for you to be able to operate at your best and achieve your targets?

List all the values on a flip chart then ask:

What is our Number One value – the one we have to operate by?

Remember to reduce your list to the top core five to six values, no more – the team must decide for themselves to achieve that loyalty and commitment to the vision.

Behaviours

So now you have your core values, it is time to take each value and get very clear on the team's behaviours to ensure there is absolute integrity between what you say and what you do.

We have completed this before with the value of trust so just repeat that exercise with every core team value to ensure you are agreed as a team and how you will behave to ensure your values are met.

Team Coaching Moment

What behaviours will we do?

 What behaviours will we not do?

Get clear and create a simple Behavioural Charter of say 10-12 behaviours that you will operate by and hold one another accountable for.

Create a succinct vision

Have all the flip charts up on the walls around the room. Take some time as a team refreshing all the work you have done.

A clear and succinct vision should be no more than five to nine words. Any more and people do not buy in, it's not memorable, and therefore it's not in the 'muscle'.

An example of this is a team I had been working with were not pulling together, struggling with their leader and not achieving their targets.

The leader had insisted they had a vision already – so they didn't need to work on it. In my pre-event interviews, it was clear there was one but no-one could remember it, no-one could say it! Consequently they had nothing to work towards to inspire and unite them. When I found it, their vision was over 20 words long and not inspirational or motivating – it was actually a strategy, not a vision and it was created by the leader alone, not the team! Once they did this exercise together they united, aligned and bought into the vision – it came alive for them.

Team Coaching Moment
create a shared vision

Having looked around at all the flip charts you have created about 'What is your vision of success' – it will start with the words 'To be...'

So keep going until you get your vision down to under nine words. Ensure it's a positive and future statement which is stretching and challenging and which you can remember and say easily and quickly and with pride. Think of some visions which excite you.

Bring it alive – visually. What will it look like? What will it feel like? What will people be saying about this team? Create a collage and get creative.

Communicating your vision – now the team need to create their elevator pitch to ensure it's consistent and can be said to your key influencers in one minute.

Team Coaching Moment
Elevator Pitch

Imagine you are in a lift with the most influential person in your organisation or your most critical customer and you have just 60 seconds to impress them – what would you say?

Ensure it incorporates:

- Who you are, your role and what you do

- Your vision and values

- Your core purpose

- What you do

This is the message that will ensure you are always prepared when you meet that critical stakeholder.

Team Coaching Moment

Each of the team members needs to do this mind map for their own part of the business (see Part One - Chapter Three page 59).

Now each person will present their elevator pitch to the team. The team will then give them feedback until everyone is confident in their own pitch.

We did this exercise for a global team who were having a change of ownership and senior leadership to prepare them so they were ready to influence their new owners and management. It made a huge difference and demonstrated succinctly that they knew what they were doing. It is surprising when you ask even senior people 'What do you do?' how much they mumble, trip over their words and are not ready with a clear succinct statement. Don't let that be you – ensure you are all prepared.

Now you have a core purpose, shared vision, shared values and a commitment to the behaviours you will do and not do. You also have an elevator pitch. You are ready to communicate this to your wider team and cascade the message. It all needs to be brought alive for your whole team or organisation to ensure that everyone is bought-in to the shared vision and values. That way you will not waste time, make the wrong decisions, hire or retain the wrong people or start your journey without the buy-in.

Team Coaching Moment
Communicate your Message

How will the team do that?

How will you achieve the buy-in of your teams?

What will you do?

When will you do it?

Each team leader should do the same exercises with their own teams.

Ensure you bring the wider teams together and maybe organise some road shows or town hall meetings.

Cascade it throughout your organisation, reflect it back at every meeting and ensure you always check in to ensure how you are doing.

Have the 'right' conversations to ensure success.

Transforming a team will take time and a commitment by you, the leader, and by every person in the team.

Summary

1. Leader shares their vision of success.

2. The team share their vision of success.

3. The team create a shared and succinct vision.

4. Elicit and agree the core purpose of the team.

5. Elicit and agree the team's shared values.

6. Agree the critical behaviours to support the values.

7. Prepare the team's elevator pitches and practise them.

8. Cascade and communicate throughout your organisation.

Chapter Four

Manage Conflict

Many individuals and cultures including our own find it difficult to have open and honest conversations and to just say it how it is. We learn how to manage conflict from a very early age. We are taught how to deal with issues by the cultures we live in and experience, our parents, our teachers and the situations we have experienced. They can embed limiting beliefs like:

- Treat others how you would like to be treated

- Don't make a fuss

- It will go away – brush it under the carpet

- It's not worth causing trouble

- Don't upset others

As a result, we soon learn to avoid conflict and not say when we are hurt or annoyed. We can learn to 'go quiet' or 'give in' and only say parts of what we want to say. The way we manage conflict is taught to us and we build our preferences based on the situations that have happened to us and the results we have had.

'Elephants in rooms' or 'monkeys on your shoulders' are very dangerous in any team. It is like a 'silent' cancer forming and spreading through the fibre of the team. These will eventually destroy any trust or respect. They poison relationships and they will cause the team and the individuals to fail at some level – if not now, at some point in the future. People leave teams and organisations because of them – so please do not let this happen to your team.

Research has proven that the ability to resolve conflict openly and constructively is one the most critical differentiators between high- and low-performing teams.

Team Coaching Moment
Conflict Management

Refer back to the team's vision and values:

- What is important to this team in the way it manages conflict?

- What limiting beliefs does this team have about how it manages conflict?

- What are you going to do differently?

A team must be able to reach agreement, make decisions and support each other to achieve their goals. However, every individual has different preferences for how they handle conflict.

To find out your team's preferences, use *Thomas Kilman Conflict Indicator* (TKI*)

The model shows that there are five key modes/preferences, depending on how assertive you are and how cooperative you are in a given situation.

In new teams the TKI* helps the team members get to know one another's conflict styles and identify potential challenges.

In established teams the TKI* helps the existing members understand the different conflict behaviours that occur within a team.

* 'TKi' is the copyright of Xicom, Inc. 1996. Xicom, Inc. is a subsidiary of CPP, Inc.

Effective conflict management is good in a team because it:

- Allows conflicts to surface and the team to resolve issues

- Produces better-quality decision-making

- Improves learning and innovation by working through issues

- Removes tension

- Strengthens work relationships and cohesiveness

- Builds trust and respect

If it is not handled effectively then:

- Poor decision-making/deadlocks will occur

- Time and energy can be wasted

- Group cohesiveness can be undermined

- A lack of trust and respect can form and breed

- Lack of commitment and accountability can result

Use the TKI* to understand your team's preferences and the strengths, challenges and gaps which arise as a result. Once you know those you can agree an effective conflict management process for your team.

* 'TKi' is the copyright of Xicom, Inc. 1996. Xicom, Inc. is a subsidiary of CPP, Inc.

Remember the dysfunctional team I wrote about earlier? Their leader avoided conflict and did everything possible to avoid having the 'right' conversation.

We used the TKI* to identify the individuals' preferred conflict management styles.

The team had a discussion about their strengths and their gaps. They were able to highlight how they could manage conflict better and create a robust conflict management strategy. The leader was able to articulate how he would stretch himself to have the conversations that he needed to have in a timely manner with each member of the team and in team meetings. The team could set aside time to discuss all the 'elephants' in their office – and theirs was quite a herd!

The TKI* is available through us at Vi International or your organisation may have access to it. Like the other psychometrics, you may need a professional facilitator to assist you.

* 'TKi' is the copyright of Xicom, Inc. 1996. Xicom, Inc. is a subsidiary of CPP, Inc.

Have the right conversation

Let me ask you this question: Would you go into a restaurant and sit down order your meal and, when it came, find the plates were dirty from a previous meal?

No, you wouldn't, would you? You would insist on clean plates.

This is effectively what you are doing when you do not have the 'right' conversation, when you only say 10% of what you want to say, when you 'avoid' the topic you need to speak to them about, when you avoid their emails and calls or when you give in to their demands just for an easy life. Or maybe you go into attack mode to get what you want and try to bulldoze your ideas through not listening to anyone's ideas or thoughts. Which one are you?

It is like trying to have a current conversation when all the time there is another conversation going on in our heads (which is the one we really want to have). You know that feeling when perhaps you have had a strong disagreement with someone and the next time you see them and they don't mention it, they just pretend it has never happened and carry on another discussion. All the time you are thinking to yourself 'Mmm – I don't trust them, why aren't they mentioning it? I expect they think I think it has gone away – well, it has not ...'

You are not listening to them but to your own internal dialogue.

It is therefore vital for the health and well-being of a team and the relationships within the team that you have the right conversation with the right person in the right way.

Clean your plates

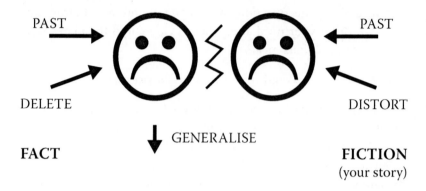

PAST → ← PAST

DELETE   DISTORT

GENERALISE

FACT   **FICTION**
                           (your story)

What was said exactly? What was done precisely? What is the exact truth? What are the facts?	LIST THE FACTS
What is the problem between you? How long have you had it? What/who caused it? Now: What exactly happened? What are you assuming? What have you deleted/distorted/generalised? What is your part in this? How are you making 'them' wrong?	LIST YOUR LIMITING BELIEFS AND BEHAVIOURS

If this carries on, what will you **gain**?	If this carries on, what will you **lose**?	**WHAT DO YOU WANT? WHAT IS YOUR OUTCOME?**

Team Coaching Moment

Clean the plates.

Pre-work

Each person to take some self-time prior to the team meeting.

Analyse and benchmark your team relationships as in Part One - Chapter Three - page 50

Ask yourself 'What conversation do I need to have with my colleague in order to improve the relationship we have? What needs to be discussed?'

Use this structure to help you analyse the relationship:

· How has the past affected your relationship now?

· What meaning did you make?

· What interpretations did you make?

· What do you want? What is your outcome?

This model will help you to understand what is and what is not working in this relationship. It will enable you to focus on your outcome and what you want.

Making someone else wrong, justifying our own thoughts and beliefs and making huge assumptions about someone else is human behaviour. If we continue with this attitude, however, we will cause our relationships to fail. The energy in the relationship disappears, there is no vitality and we stop saying what we should say. Eventually the relationship dies.

In teams we do not have that option – we have to work alongside our peers and to work on building strong relationships.

Building strong relationships requires building empathy and rapport. It is about understanding someone else's perspective. This next exercise helps you to do that so that you can experience a situation from many different viewpoints so that you can gain insight and, therefore, information to help you.

Team Coaching Moment
Understanding perspectives

Take any challenging stakeholder or team relationship and work through the following steps to achieve a deeper understanding.

Step One	Being You	Sit in your shoes	What is your perspective?
Step Two	Being Them	Sit in their shoes	What is their perspective?
Step Three	Observer	Detach yourselves	What is the impartial perspective?
Step Four	Expert	Detach/ advise	What would the expert say to do?

Take all the information from all perspectives

Step Five	Being You	Sit in your shoes	What is your position now?
			What actions will you take?
			What outcome do you want?

	You	Ano	
1st			2nd

3rd	Observer	Expert	4th

We tend to only 'sit' in our own position (Position 1) and not be able to move ourselves literally into another's (Position 2) shoes. If we stay in Position 1 we only see the 'issue' from our eyes. This gives us only a small percentage of information and a very 'blinkered' view. If you are always thinking of someone else and their position (2) and how they are feeling, you will never get what you want. If you are always a detached observer (3) then you will never feel what it really feels like to achieve success and the joy that comes from that. If you are always the expert (4) on everything then you will never bring people along with you.

Understanding different perspectives will bring you a heightened emotional intelligence and give you a different perspective to enable you to achieve the success you want.

Remember 'perception is projection' – the perception you have of the other person/people is often what you are projecting on to them. This causes a deep resentment on others because they pick up from you what you are really thinking.

I remember a team in an organisation which was being taken over by another with completely different values. The team were at 'effect' and therefore giving all the power to their 'stakeholders'.

Their conversation and mindset was 'wasting their time and energy' consistently talking about 'them' and how difficult 'they' were, how challenging 'they' were. So to give them back their strength and power, I asked them to write on a flip chart all of their complaints about 'them', for example:

- They are aggressive

- They don't listen

- They don't respect us

- They don't trust us

- They are not good communicators

Then I asked them to change the 'they' into 'we' and the 'us' into 'them':

- **We** are aggressive

- **We** don't listen

- **We** don't respect them

- **We** don't trust them

- **We** are not good communicators

It was an amazing realisation that this team had and it enabled them to think more creatively about how they could approach these issues differently.

Team Coaching Moment

Take any difficult stakeholder relationship you want to improve and ask yourselves these questions:

What is your perception of them?

What are you projecting on to them?

What are you going to do differently to improve these relationships?

It gives you a great reminder that by giving power to someone else you are projecting that negativity on to them and causing a lot of your own problems. Stop now.

Team Coaching Moment
Have the right conversations – just say it

Organise to bring the team together for a minimum of half a day and preferably know your own TKI* profiles so that you can share them. This will help the conversations and to understand the different behaviours. If you are in a global team then ensure that these 'big' conversations happen when you are face-to-face and definitely before you fly home.

Pre-work

Prior to the meeting, ask everyone to come prepared as follows:

· What are the top five 'big issues' that we have in this team?

· What are the top five challenges that we have right now?

· What is not working in this team that we need to change now?

At every team dynamics meeting it is important to refer back to your vision and your values so that the spirit of the team remains alive. This gives the team the security that they can be honest and open and they can say what they feel. It is especially important for those sessions as it is talking about everything that is difficult every day that's not working – it is 'peeling off the layers of the onion' to really find out what the team's core issues are.

So it is vital to create a place of 'safety' and confidentiality – maybe take time off-site into a relaxed environment where everyone can talk freely.

Remember before you start to talk this through to say 'It's OK, there are no wrong answers, everything you say is important and has a value so don't hold back.' You need to be brave and patient and you need to listen. Don't ignore it and don't avoid it.

Team Coaching Moment

Team discussion

Put every issue on to a flip chart. What is the Number One issue we need to resolve today? Go through the list until you have a clear list of the top five issues. Any more than that and you have not got to the core issues. Then ask yourselves each of the questions below on each of the issues.

Exercise

Questions:

- What is the outcome we want?

- Who do we need to influence?

- What will be our evidence of success?

- What resources do we have to help us?

- What actions do we need to take?

- How could we stop our own success?

- What will we do differently?

- What is our first step to resolving this?

Be open, stretch yourselves and take each issue and define your outcome and your route to success.

What if you have a very challenging relationship?

Sometimes a team is fractured by one or two people just not getting along for a number of reasons. Some go back a long way, some just happen over a series of misunderstandings, some are easily improved whilst others will require more work and some courageous conversations by both parties.

Team Coaching Moment

Each team member to analyse the relationship he/she has with each of their colleagues. Benchmark them now and what your outcome is for three months' time. Take the most challenging relationship and prepare yourself.

1. Get clear on the outcome you want – use this model.

2. Get clear on the problems between you:

    a. What exactly has caused this situation?

    b. How long has this situation been going on?

    c. What behaviours need to change on both sides?

3. Get clear on what 'you' want in this situation:

    a. Take ownership and responsibility – what is your part in this?

    b. How are you 'making' this worse?

    c. What are your judgements/opinions and complaints about 'them'?

We spend a lot of time and energy making someone else wrong, building up issues and lists of everything wrong with them. We even seek out opinions and data from others to justify our own beliefs and try to make ourselves right. We continue with this inside ourselves and build up and create our own 'soap opera' that actually has little to do with the fact of the situation. Remember the 'clean plates' exercise.

One of my coachees had a difficult situation with his boss which had been building for a few weeks. He had started to make meaning of what she had said which had no resemblance of the 'actual' and 'factual' words spoken. By the time the last event happened he was sure he was going to lose his job. He had prepared a presentation for her and was given the feedback 'OK, can you double-check it again for any typos' – that is all she said. He then made the decision 'She doesn't rate me, she's going to sack me – I'd better find another job.' He then went home later that night with his self-speak turned on with this going on and on in his head. He got into his car and promptly went and scraped three cars in the car park! He had made it up – he had created huge stresses in his body which caused this accident. A true story, so be aware we all do this but to have healthy relationships you must try and stop it.

Ask yourself 'What meaning am I making of this situation/ comment?' 'What exactly happened which can be proven in a Court of Law – if we played it back and observed it?'

If you are having one-to-one coaching you can always ask yourself and discuss with your coach:

Who does this person remind me of?

Where in my past does this reaction belong?

What value is their behaviour in conflict with?

Where does this relationship issue come from?

That information is worth knowing because we often blame people in the present for what's happened to us in the past. People can remind us of significant people who have 'hurt' us way back then.

I remember a time when I was presenting to one of the largest advertising companies in the world and the HR director introduced me as 'Nicky'. I felt personally violated because I am never called Nicky. I felt my body language change, my breathing became quicker and higher. My mind raced ahead of me – then I had to present my work. I recovered enough but afterwards I sat and wondered just why I had had that severe reaction to one word. I thought about where this had happened before and my mind took me back to a very unpleasant situation at school when I was about 16. When I took myself back there I could feel exactly the feelings I had just experienced. Every memory is attached to the neural and physical networks in your body and it will cause a reaction.

That's where one-to-one executive coaching can ensure you clear yourself and your team of any past negative experiences. This will fast-track a team to success, especially if it is underperforming, new, or has stretching targets to achieve.

It's also important for the team to have well-structured, meaningful discussions at the right level to avoid any misunderstanding and cause any issues. To do this it is vital to have adult-to-adult conversations.

Transactional Analysis is a theory of personality originated by Eric Berne and can provide useful insights for personal growth and change in a team.

Everyone has different levels of thinking, feeling and behaving. One of the systems that Berne introduces is Parent, Adult and Child ego states. Understanding these systems and how they affect our behaviour and communication with others gives opportunities for choice.

There are many books available on TA or the team will require a trained facilitator to help them. In brief, we all have Parent/ Adult and Child ego states within us. Sometimes we operate in one more than another. An example of this is a leader with whom I have worked predominantly in 'Controlling Parent' and therefore pushing his team into 'Rebellious Child' and not having adult conversations. The effect of this was the team took no responsibility, he took more and more control treating them more and more like 'children' and they were not achieving their targets.

Team Coaching Moment

As a team, discuss ego states and share which one is your preferred way of operating.

Then agree: How can we ensure we improve communication within our team and with our stakeholders?

When will Nurturing Parent be useful?

When will Controlling Parent be useful?

When will Rebellious Child be useful?

When will Natural Child be useful?

When will Adult be useful?

I remember when we did this with another team; they were not achieving targets either.

The Leader was mostly in 'Controlling Parent'.

The team and their teams were mainly in 'Rebellious or Adapted Child'.

This led to a culture of 'fear', conforming and a feeling they were being watched all the time and not trusted or good enough. They responded by not getting on the telephone, by not going out to see the customers and staying stuck to their desks.

Once the leader had heard and listened to the feedback, she changed behaviour, the team challenged her more, they had more adult-to-adult conversations, they took more ownership and cascaded this through their teams. The behaviour started to change, the culture started to change into one of responsibility and ownership with a focus on results.

It is equally important to have one-to-one conversations in the best ego state so that you do not get crossed communication and misunderstanding. So before any 'challenging' conversation remember to move your thinking into the most appropriate 'mindset'.

Now you are prepared to have the 'right' conversation and achieve your outcome.

It's important to ensure the environment is conducive to the conversation, so not in your office or theirs – ideally get out of the office. Ensure the other person knows why you want to see them – be open but don't get pulled into any details before the meeting.

Maybe you could say 'I recognise we have had a few challenging situations recently and I would like to get together and work out with you how we can work together better in the future.'

When you meet up, do take time to build rapport. Remember, rapport is pacing their body language and voice energy. Now have the conversation.

Coaching Moment - prepare

Step 1   Build rapport.

Step 2   Focus on the 'future' relationship you want to have
                – your outcome.

Step 3   Recognise the 'past' relationship has not always
                been successful. Get clear on the
                reason/s why. State 'how' you hold yourself
                responsible and for 'what'. State 'what' you will be
                doing differently in the future.

Step 4   Recognise their strengths/contributions and value.
                State what behaviour you would like them to start
                doing more of in the future.

Step 5   Ask them for feedback and a feedforward for you.
                Listen and take it on board.

Step 6   Agree 'how' you will build your relationship.

                Agree what you will both do differently.

                Agree on what your evidence of success will be.

                Agree 'how' to give one another ongoing feedback/
                feedforward.

Feedback is important for growth and development. However, it focuses on what has already occurred in the past and not on the vast possibilities of the future. Feedforward, however, gives suggestions for the future in a helpful and supportive manner whilst focusing on making a positive difference going forward. Feeding forward is essential for growth and it has been proven that our brains process a positive message better than a negative one.

The principles of feedforward

We can change the future – we can't change the past

It can be more productive to help people be 'right' than prove they were 'wrong'

Feedforward is suited to successful people

Feedforward can come from anyone at any time

People do not take feedforward as personally as feedback

Easy to give feedforward suggestions

Feedforward tends to be much faster and more efficient than feedback

Team Coaching Moment
Feedforward technique

- Each team member chooses ONE behaviour that they would like to change which will make a positive difference

- State this behaviour 'I want to ...'

- Ask for feedforward – two suggestions for the future that might help you make a positive change in their selected behaviour

- Listen attentively and without judgement to their suggestions

- Say thank you for the suggestions

Identify the behavioural change you want to make.

Now use this when building key relationships.

Remember too that feedback/feedforward should always be given at a behavioural level (what they do). So you would say something like 'I noticed when both you and Catherine were discussing the recent problem we have had with customer service that the body language and tone of voice used was not consistent with what was being said' rather than 'I noticed that when you and Catherine were discussing the problem we have with customer service that your body language and your tone of voice was inconsistent with what you said.'

It is better to keep your feedback and feedforward at a behavioural level – what the behaviour is – and give examples at that level.

In my experience, everyone likes to hear what they do well when it is said honestly and freely, and examples given. They also want to know how they can get better and develop further.

No one, in my experience, intentionally wants to upset or hurt another human being. Often this occurs because of different cultures, different values, different personality traits and different conversational styles.

So remember some good NLP (Neuro Linguistic Programming) tips:

'There are no difficult people only inflexible communicators'

So how can you communicate differently?

'There is always a positive intention behind every negative behaviour'

So what is that positive intention?

'There is no failure – only feedback'

So what can you learn and do differently?

'There is a solution to every problem'

So keep looking.

'Separate people from their behaviour – behaviour is what people do not who they are'

So what is the behaviour?

Have the conversations you need to have with every one of your direct reports and ensure that you all have the conversations you need to have with each another.

'Clean your plates' and keep them clean – check regularly.

Have the 'trust' conversations with each of your critical stakeholders in the same way.

Be brave and have the conversations with your boss. To be a truly great leader, that will involve influencing upwards as well as down and across your organisation.

Be even braver and have them now with the people you know you need to have them with. It will be like the conversation I had with my Dad which made the difference that changed my relationship with him.

Go now before it's too late, and if you need more in-depth help, then hire a coach to help you prepare.

Summary

1. Agree 'How the team will manage conflict' aligned with the vision and values.

2. Elicit the team's limiting beliefs about how to manage conflict.

3. Use the TKI* for each team member:

   a.   Identify strengths and capabilities

   b.   Agree conflict management strategy

4. What are the top five big issues?

   a.   What are the top five big challenges?

   b.   And agree action plan

5. Build all team relationships:

   a.   Benchmark

   b.   Complete relationship outcomes

6. Have the difficult conversations:

   a.   'Clean your plates'

   b.   Define your outcomes

7. Give feedback and feedforward.

8. Use TA to have adult-to-adult conversations.

---

* 'TKi' is the copyright of Xicom, Inc. 1996. Xicom, Inc. is a subsidiary of CPP, Inc.

PART THREE

Achieving Targets

Chapter One

Plan for Success

'Failure to plan is planning to fail' and it is so true isn't it?

If you've skipped Part One and Part Two then that is what you are doing now – planning to fail. Don't think that you can achieve your targets if you have not built a winning team and if you have not developed yourself; it won't work. You can't 'short circuit' to success. So go back now and do what you can from all the hints and tips you will find to help you fast-track.

It's easy to think that all you have to do is work hard and keep 'doing', and work harder and harder, later and later, until it's taking all weekend. That isn't the answer. Something is going very wrong if that is what you are doing and this is why it is vital to start this process by:

Knowing Yourself

By understanding and knowing exactly who you are, what motivates and drives you, what your purpose and vision is. By exploring your personality traits, how you work at your best with your top strengths, what your gaps are and what you can do to develop them, you will be a much better leader and able to transform your team to achieve great results.

Knowing Your Team

By working together with your team and creating a shared vision, common values and principles and tapping into your strengths, you will be working together building trust, loyalty, respect, commitment and accountability. You will be discussing the issues that could stop you and you will also be talking through any relationship issues in the team ensuring that there are no 'elephants' or 'monkeys' between you.

That means you have put in the critical steps to building a winning team – a team that performs at its best all the time with everyone.

Now you can focus on ensuring you achieve the targets – no doubt very ambitious targets like every other business has today.

These targets are huge and can seem unachievable, and virtually impossible – but if you continue thinking that way, that's exactly what they will be.

Changing the 'mindset' of the team is vital – if they believe it's impossible and difficult, that is what they will be saying to their people. If they do that, then guess what – everyone is saying it and believes it and so the climate of failure is born. Change your thinking – change your results!

The key to success is to ensure that the culture you are creating in your organisation and every team within it is a culture of success, a winning culture, a climate that is determined to achieve – and never ever give up.

Teams need to:

• Stay focused on success and aware of what could stop them

• Be flexible in their thoughts and behaviours so they can change direction if they need to

• Build strong networks, both internally and externally

• Be proactive and take action

That is how Vi International has been able to survive and thrive – everyone has committed to the vision and lives by our values. We spend our time where it is best spent – with our clients and delegates. We focus 100% on our customers and their needs. We don't have huge offices; we don't spend on anything we don't need so that we don't have to pass the cost on to our clients. We have managed to keep our costs down and ensure our clients benefit from that too. We do invest in our development because it is what makes us the 'best' coaches and better than our competitors. We continue to focus on 'success not failure'.

I remember an organisation which was taken over by a new leader. It was not achieving targets and was failing in many areas. It had been 'leaderless' for about six months and all they were doing was working 'day to day', fire fighting, dealing with the issues as they happened. There was no vision of success. The climate was negative with low morale, low engagement and no energy or commitment.

The leader took about two years to turn it around. He got to know his team and gradually restructured and built the team. Together they created a culture of success by doing everything that I have laid out in this guide. They communicated their vision with clarity and passion throughout and achieved buy-in from their whole organisation. They faced their issues, then they sold the business for a huge amount – what an amazing result for all of the team. Their return on investment was £6 for every £1 – an incredible result.

So that's what can be done if you are determined – you can turn around a failing organisation/team as long as you stay focused on what is important.

There are five steps to achieving your targets that I have found to make a difference and which are used by successful people and successful teams I have worked with:

Know your outcome

Know exactly what you want to achieve and know what your evidence is of success.

Build strong relationships with your team, your whole organisation, your key stakeholders and your clients/customers – build rapport.

Be very aware

See what you need to see.

Hear what you need to hear.

Gather information and keep focused on your goals.

Be flexible

As you gather information, be ready to move and change course should you need to. Don't stay stuck doing the same old things.

What behavioural strategy are you 'stuck' in? What do you need to do differently?

Be proactive

Take action and stop being reactive, and don't procrastinate.

What are you not doing on a daily basis that if you did do would make a difference to your results?

Get out there and just do it.

Step 1 - Know Your Outcome

When studies were done of high performers by Robert Dilts in his book *Strategies of Genius – people* who have achieved great things in their work, like Aristotle, Mozart and Walt Disney – he found they used their minds in a certain way. This is still found to be consistent today with people like Richard Branson and the late Steve Jobs. The NLP outcome model can help you reframe your thinking and help you to success. Use the model overleaf to ensure you have a well-formed outcome.

Team Coaching Moment

Take your top three targets.

Work through a detailed outcome model for each target.

1 OUTCOME
What do you want to achieve?
What will that do for you?

2 EVIDENCE OF SUCCESS
Your evidence for having achieved the outcome:
What will you see, hear, feel? What will you be doing when you are being successful?

3 TAKING ACTION
What are the top 10 things you must do now?
What could stop you?

4 RESOURCES/STRENGTHS
What strengths does the team have to be successful?
What 'other' resources are available now?

5 SPECIFICS
Who do you need to influence?
What are the milestones to success?

6 CHECK IN
What will you gain if you succeed?
What will you lose?

Is it worth the time/cost of what it will take?

I've used this model to build Vi International and I've used it many times in my private life to help me face the most enormous obstacles; without this model, I wouldn't have found the strength and resources to continue at times.

It's vital for you to get very clear on the targets and objectives that you need to achieve before you bring your team together by using this model.

Step 2 - Build your Relationships

Know exactly what you have to achieve by the year end.

Get very clear.

Get so clear that you can visualise it in detail, that you can 'be there' in the future having achieved it. That way you will be inspiring and motivating.

Be very clear on who you need to influence to achieve these objectives and use the relationship benchmark tool as below:

Manager	*Stakeholders*
Direct Reports	*Peer Group*

Each member of your team should get clear on their stakeholders.

Be very specific on what resources you already have that will help you achieve your targets.

List down all the actions you need to take to achieve your results.

Know exactly what could stop you achieving success and also know how you could stop yourself. This is an important part of the process. Disney called it his 'critic' stage. Once you've assessed everything that could stop you, then take each one and ask yourself:

What do I need to do to solve this issue?

and if it's 'you'

What belief do I need to believe instead so I don't stop myself?

Get clear on what you will gain/lose/how much time it will take and how much investment is required to achieve your targets.

As you are now aware, it's critical that you are well prepared before bringing your team together – so by doing this piece of self-preparation you will be ready.

It's also important to have one-to-ones with each of your team to go through their targets and objectives so they are clear. It's your responsibility to ensure they understand exactly what their roles and responsibilities are and exactly what you are expecting of them by the year end.

It is vital that this is done as soon as possible at the beginning of the year – don't wait until Q2 as some leaders do and then expect an engaged and motivated team.

So once you bring the team together, everyone knows their objective and targets for the year ahead.

You now have many tools to help you build strong relationships with each of your team, but don't forget to apply these to your key stakeholders/customers and even your leader.

The FiroB* (Fundamental Interpersonal Relationship Orientation to Behaviour) is a powerful psychometric which gives information about how individuals deal with their interpersonal relationships. This can be used effectively when bringing a new or underperforming team together or when a team needs to build their stakeholder relationships. It has to be administered by a qualified facilitator and your organisation may have access to this. It will tell you what strengths the team have and what they need to develop and be aware of in order to build strong relationships.

Build a Performance Culture

You know how important that is and now you can start the process and cascade it throughout your organisation/team. Communicating your vision is vital and it is critical to bring people together so that you can achieve this quickly.

I remember an NHS PCT who cascaded and communicated their vision and values and had asked their organisation for feedback. They organised some 'whole organisation' events

* Firo-B is a registered trademark of CPP Inc

and brought people together on three-hour sessions out of their place of work. This had never been done before and the feedback was phenomenal; and over the four years they went from a £18m deficit to a £22m profit. Staff engagement increased significantly.

So it can be done if you change the culture.

Don't ignore the 'big' issues – talk them through, make decisions and take action to remedy.

Don't have 'elephants and monkeys' in the room – discuss in depth.

Don't stop yourselves – change your limiting beliefs.

Don't do 'negative' behaviours – change them – it starts with you, remember?

Success takes planning. So stop and plan and get clear about your objectives then bring the plan together.

Give them some pre-work to do, as follows:

Come prepared to share with the team your targets and objectives for this year and ask them to share this at the start of the day – include yourself in this exercise so they know what you have to achieve.

Ask them:

What are your challenges to achieving your targets?

What support do you need from the team?

Take the time with your team, to discuss as a team, what the targets are and how you are going to achieve them.

Take time to listen to their concerns and their needs.

Mentor and coach them to success.

Summary

1. 'Change the Mindset' and 'Change the Culture'.

2. Know your outcomes:

    Targets

3. Influence who you need to influence – analyse:

    Stakeholders

    Team

4. Build strong relationships:

    Employees

    Customers

5. Have one-to-ones with each direct report:

    Get clear on targets

    Review and check in

    Coach for success

6. Build a performance culture:

    Give feedback

    Give feedforward

    Discuss the big issues

    Change limiting beliefs

    Coach for success

Chapter Two

Set all your Targets

It's not just about financial targets. So many leaders make a huge mistake in thinking it is all that is important; some organisations make a similar mistake by only rewarding the achievement of financial targets. It is not; and in all my years of developing leaders and teams, people are not motivated only by money. In fact, many people are not motivated at all by money. That's why it's vital to elicit your team's values. You need to know what motivates them and what demotivates them or they will not achieve their targets

It's also about 'how' you will achieve your targets. It's how you 'lead' your people; it's how your customers are treated.

People are generally motivated by their 'super' values of freedom, safety and happiness' and want to be treated with respect and dignity. They want to be trusted and to work with people they can trust. They want to have open and honest conversations. They want to enjoy their time at work. So in order to achieve your results you need to think about setting your leadership targets and objectives as well as your financial metrics.

There are three core areas to think about when you bring your team together:

1. What are our targets for our customers?

2. What are our targets for our shareholders?

3. What are our targets for our employees?

Start with an exercise taking each area in turn and establish where you are now.

What is the current reality?

What exactly is your score now? (if 0 is low and 10 is high and measure success.) Maybe you already have organisational tools that can do this for you.

What exactly is **not** working now?

What precisely **is** working now?

Collate as much information as possible which gives you the data you need so that you can monitor your success. If you don't have that information then ensure you invest in purchasing tools which will enable it. You must know:

1. Where you are now.

2. What's working well.

3. What you have to change.

Organisations spend millions on staff engagement surveys and customer loyalty surveys etc. but often their leaders do not use them to their fullest potential to help them achieve their objectives.

If your company has them, then be sure to use them and be sure to also think about 'how' you will lead your people.

Team Coaching Moment

As a team – get clear and assess your present position then use this following exercise 'Steps to Success' to ensure you succeed. It is important to do the exercise in the order that it is explained; that way you will not get hung up on trying to see your way from the tough position you may be in.

1	2	3	4	5
Current Reality	First Steps	Half Way Stage	Nearly There	End of Year Evidence of Success
Date:	Date:	Date:	Date:	Date:
Where are you now? What's working? What's not? Know your outcomes	Now: What are you going to do now? What are your first steps? What has to be completed by: Step 3? Step 4? Step 5?	To have achieved Box 5 where do you need to be here? What do you have to have achieved? Who have you influenced? What have you got to do now?	To have achieved your targets what do you have to do now? What do you have to stop doing? What do you have to start doing? Go to 2	What exactly will you have achieved? Leadership goals Financial What are your measures of success? Define them How will this feel? Go to 3
What could stop you? How does this feel? Go to 5	What are you going to stop doing? What are you going to start doing? Who do you need to influence?	How are you stopping yourselves? Go to 4		

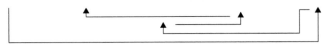

Team Coaching Moment

Create the future success

Take each of the areas as before and get clear on the crucial measures of success for each core area: Customer, Stakeholder and Employee.

Each person in the team must be included and give their input. Get clear.

Exercise:

1. Use flip charts, artistic materials, colour and get creative.

2. Map out the time line on the floor – yes, physically do it. Past – Present – Future.

3. All walk into the future and position flip chart at one end. This is where you are standing.

4. Start with the 'end in mind' as Stephen Covey says in *The 7 Habits of Highly Effective People*. This is great pre-reading for your team.

5. Imagine you are celebrating success in this financial year. You have achieved all your objectives and you have hit target. Act 'as if' you are a year older or however long it is to your year end.

    Stay with the future in your mind.

Act 'as if' you have been successful from this place.

What have you achieved?

What can you see happening?

What can you hear being said?

What recognition have you got?

6. Create a storyboard of what success is as a team.

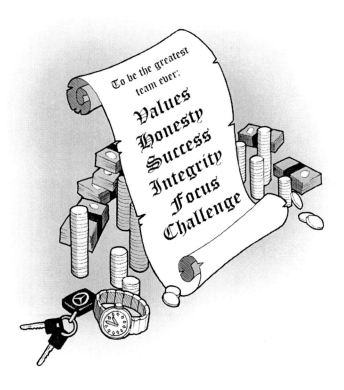

7. Bring that information back to the present on the time line and ask yourselves as a team:

What do we have to do now to ensure that we are successful?

What is the number one thing we have to do?

Get SMART?

Specific

Measurable

Achievable

Realistic

Time-bound

8. What do we have to stop doing now?

Now take a break.

The final part of the exercise, after a break, is to:

1. Ask:

   a. What past experiences can we draw on to ensure our success?

   b. What do we want to take forward?

   c. What knowledge do we want to keep?

2. Bring everything back to the present – you know what success and reaching targets looks like; what resources from the past and present you need to keep and where you are now and what you need to do in the present to ensure you are successful as a team.

So just do it.

Bring the team together.

Create a compelling future.

I remember a team in India who did this exercise. I have never experienced such a tremendous positive spirit as it caused. The team changed from being a low-energy team, fearful of sharing, not knowing one another, to quite the opposite – a senior team brought together, being creative and creating their successful future – and they did.

Now your team knows its targets, its objectives and what it has to do to get there. It knows its vision of success. Now it is vital to get commitment and accountability for each person in the team referring back to their own targets and objectives.

Team Coaching Moment

Just ask these questions:

What are you commitments to this team's success?

What support do you need to achieve your targets and objectives?

What support do you offer your colleagues to ensure their success?

How can the team hold you accountable?

Each member of the team, including the leader, must take time to prepare (allow a minimum of 30 minutes each). When they come back, allow at least 10 minutes each for the team to share their commitments and accountability statements – get these documented on to flip charts!

That way you have put in place and the team has committed to achieving their targets and what support the team needs – you have started to create a successful future. Now all you have to do is create a culture to support this right through this team here and also your wider teams. If you do this, then everyone is working for success, they are not stopping themselves or one another but really pulling together.

Summary

1. Set your targets – customer, shareholder and employees.

2. Know your leadership goals and your financial goals.

3. Establish your current reality in regard to all of the above.

4. Complete the 'Steps to Success' on all goals.

5. Create a compelling future.

6. Agree support required.

7. Achieve commitment and accountability.

Chapter Three

Create a Performance Culture

'There is no failure only feedback'

If you are to reach your targets and your objectives year on year in a challenging climate then it is vital that you create a culture which is focused on high performance in your team. We know from recent studies by The Hay Group that:

- 26% of leaders create a high-performing culture

- Revenue growth is 2.5 times greater with high levels of employee engagement

- There is 40% reduction in staff turnover when teams are motivated and engaged

- Less than two-thirds of employees believe they are as productive as they could be

- Motivation and enablement drives performance and it is real leadership that makes the difference

Poor performance in a team is down to poor leadership from the top. It is up to you as the top team to lead, motivate and engage your people. Poor leadership leads to poor results.

In my experience there are five key areas to ensuring that you create a performance culture in your team:

One: Agree targets (Part Three, Chapter One) – be clear on your objectives, roles and responsibilities.

Two: Give and seek feedback (Part Three, Chapter Two) – ensure your teams know and understand their strengths and development areas and are given opportunities 'to develop'.

Three: Give your people the tools to lead and coach their people to perform and succeed (Part Three, Chapter Two).

Four: Build a team identity and brand (Part Two, Chapter Three) – knowing your identity, purpose, vision, values and focus on employees' strengths – and communicate and cascade it.

Five: Celebrate success (Part Three, Chapter Four) – give recognition. Employees are motivated when they are part of a successful team. Successful teams celebrate success.

Performance improves with great feedback and creating a coaching culture running through the DNA of the organisation.

As we have said before, our society has embedded a fear of feedback. Some models that are used in businesses today just don't work and as a result we dread the word 'feedback'. What we also know is that people do want to know what they do well, when they have done something which has made a positive difference and what value they bring to a team/organisation. We also know that we are not perfect, we are going to make mistakes but we will learn from them if we allow ourselves.

We learn the most from the most difficult issues/challenges that we have had – as long as we take the time to stop and think and remember what we have learned that was positive for us.

So generally people are open to knowing what they can do better, that they need to develop, as long as it's done in a way that is constructive and not destructive. People want to develop, they want to get better and ultimately it is said by psychologists that a person 'strives to be the best version of themselves' – so it's up to you as a great leader to ensure people in your organisation are given that gift.

That's why we at Vi International use the word 'feedforward'. This gives feedback in a positive, constructive way and ensures someone knows exactly what they need to do to be successful.

Make it easy for the team – start with you.

Leader Coaching Moment

Go back to Part One 'Be Yourself' and review your learnings. Ask for feedback about three to four months after you've joined a team or organisation and become their leader.

Implement a 360° process throughout your direct report team or ask an executive coach to implement it for you. That way your team, your leader and your stakeholders will know that feedback is important to you and that you want to know what you do well and what you can do better. Perhaps start with the end in mind, revert to your vision and values – you will not be successful if you don't ask for feedback and you definitely won't be successful if you don't act on it.

Team Coaching Moment

Each member of the leadership team should also ensure they do a 360° Leadership Feedback. That way you know what your people think of you and what you need to stop, start and continue doing to create success. If you do not ask, you will not know!

Agree when you will all ensure you complete the 360° process.

So now it is time to bring the team together again to continue giving feedback and feed forward to each other and to start this culture in the leadership team.

This session can be completed at the end of a business meeting or at the end of one of your team development sessions. Either way, ensure it starts now and continues and becomes a natural way of operating, so everyone knows what they are great at and what they need to work on.

Feedback is fundamental to success; we give and receive feedback all the time, either consciously or unconsciously (through our body language and other non-verbal signals like the tone of our voice). It's how we give the feedback and how we receive it that will make the difference. It means nothing if we don't do anything with it and to others it can signify that you do not think it's important and therefore they are not significant to you. So be careful when you ask for feedback, you will be expected to act on it.

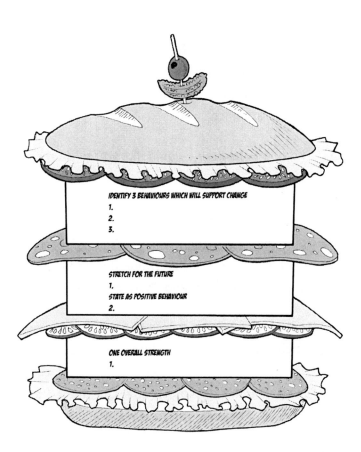

IDENTIFY 3 BEHAVIOURS WHICH WILL SUPPORT CHANGE
1.
2.
3.

STRETCH FOR THE FUTURE
1.
STATE AS POSITIVE BEHAVIOUR
2.

ONE OVERALL STRENGTH
1.

Team Coaching Moment

Pre-work – stop and think about these two questions and come prepared to share your answers with each of your colleagues:

1. What I value most in you is ...

2. What I can trust you for is ...

Map these on to a flip chart so that everyone can have a copy of these notes. It is surprising how much this means to people and it doesn't matter how senior the person is. It is rare that people are told how much they are 'valued and trusted'.

Now ask them to give a 'feedforward'. This is a stretch for the future, something you want them to develop or do differently which, if they did, would contribute significantly to the team's success and performance.

1. The one behaviour I would like you to do more of/ develop is ...

Now, if you have some significant negative and self-limiting behaviours in the team, then ask yourself, of each of your colleagues, what is the one behaviour that they do that will stop the success of the team and share as follows:

2. The one behaviour I would like you to stop doing which is affecting the performance of our team is ...

The best time to add this question is after Questions 1 and 2 and before Question 3. That way you have an effective feed forward sandwich enabling each person to develop and strengthen themselves.

We do this exercise with every team but the one I remember the most is a NHS Board which had been underperforming because of some poor behaviours by some board members.

As an organisation, the NHS in my experience does not give feedback or feedforward. Therefore negative behaviours are not spoken about and, if they are, it is not in a powerful or motivating way. Positive behaviours are not recognised and therefore no one knows what they are doing well, what they are great at and how their contribution is making a difference.

After doing this exercise, the atmosphere changed totally; for the first time they were hearing what their colleagues thought of them – positively. They also heard in a positive way how some of the behaviours they were doing were affecting the power of the team and its success. They could then change them.

Relationships were built that are still sustained today. It made a huge difference to the confidence of the team and then they cascaded it down to their teams – it became one of the key tools, which enabled them to improve their staff engagement results. So it can change cultures.

Leadership is Key

Giving people tools to lead is one of your most important roles as a leader. Your employees will be motivated and inspired if you are prepared to invest in them.

We have already covered some of the standard principles which can help them. So investigate what your organisation can offer your team which will help to develop a leadership culture. Key things in my experience are:

- MBTI* - Understanding personality

- TKI** - Conflict management

- Firo B*** – Relationship management

- 360° – ECI – Leading with emotional intelligence

- One-to-one executive leadership coaching

- Strengthscope/Strengths Finder – understanding and using strengths

- High impact presentation skills

- Leadership and coaching skills for leaders

Coaching is a vital to every team's and organisation's success. It has been proven that a coaching culture breeds success – behaviour breeds behaviour so ensure you are embedding the behaviours of success not failure. There are six steps to ensure that coaching is in your DNA.

---

* MBTI is a trademark or registered trademark of the Myers-Briggs Type Indicator Trust in the United States and other countries

** 'TKi' is the copyright of Xicom, Inc. 1996. Xicom, Inc. is a subsidiary of CPP, Inc.

*** Firo-B is a registered trademark of CPP Inc

Team Coaching Moment

Benchmark now – how are you doing? What do you need to do differently to build a culture of success?

1 Establishing a Coaching Style through the team	Ability to create a culture of success. Developing coaching skills.	Actions?
2 Active Listening	Ability to focus on what the person is saying and create shared understanding. Focuses attention on the individual's concerns, goals, values and belief system.	
3 Powerful Communication	Ability to ask questions and make statements that provide maximum benefit for a coaching interaction. Provide 'feedforward'.	
4 Creating Awareness	Ability to help employees gain awareness, leading to action and results. Explore issues to gain understanding.	

5 Action Planning and Goal Setting	Ability to create actions that will meet the individual's outcomes. Explores solutions and specific development needs.	
6 Managing Progress and Accountability	Ability to leave responsibility with the individual. Ensure they hold themselves accountable for their results. Provide ongoing support. Check in and focus on agreed actions.	

Remember, it starts in the top team. The culture of success needs to start here. Start now to create a coaching culture in your team because that is when people feel empowered and motivated to achieve their results.

These are just some of the tools available which are proven to make a difference to how your people lead and coach their people. There are many others available so ensure you use your company's resources.

Ensure that everyone has a Personal Development Plan in place and that they are provided with the tools to improve. That will make a huge difference to the motivation and enablement and therefore the performance of your team.

Team Coaching Moment

The leader asks each member of the team at a team meeting:

What do you need, want and expect from me as your leader so that you can achieve your objectives?

What will be the effect if you don't get the support you need?

Give yourselves time to do this, allow time to prepare (or this could be pre-work) – and then allow time for each person to share with you – map it on to flip charts.

The power in this is to hear everyone's contribution.

Leader Coaching Moment

Now the leader states what he needs, wants and expects of the team.

Allow time for questions after each session.

This exercise made a huge difference when we did it with a global team with a new leader (one of their former peers). It gave the team time to understand what exactly she wanted from them, what was similar and what was different from the previous leader and to give her vital information on what they expected from her as their leader. The new leader was embedded at that first event – no time was wasted trying to understand her needs, wants and expectations. This fast-tracked the team and they went on to improve all their results in that first year. The transition was seamless.

It just made it easy and effortless, even though she was a totally different leader from the previous one and she made her mark at that session.

Summary

1. Agree your targets.

2. Continually give and receive feedback.

3. Always 'feed forward'.

4. Create a coaching culture.

5. Give your people the tools to lead.

6. Build your team brand identity.

7. Ask: What do you need, want and expect from me to succeed?

8. Celebrate success.

Chapter Four

Celebrate Success

This is one area where leaders who lead high-performing teams and organisations always spend time and investment because they know it motivates and engages their people.

'Work hard, play hard' is a mantra they often say to me and I've seen them do it.

Great leaders always make the time to:

- Give verbal and written recognition when they see great performance – when they see it in the moment. If you see it, say it

- Ensure they give positive feedback during every one-to-one on what that individual has succeeded and tell them the difference that it is making to the team's success

- If they have 'failed' then coach them to success

- Take time out with the team to socialise and get to know one another – talk about the successes the team has had

- Check in every meeting to ask the team how they are doing and ensuring everyone feels valued

- Communicate, communicate, communicate everything that is important, positive and successful and that demonstrates how the team is performing

- Reward and recognise both leadership and financial targets

- Have fun with new teams – time to laugh

I remember my daughter in one of her first senior roles as a recruitment consultant with a large organisation. Eventually she became one of their 'top billers' and consistently outperformed the rest. The CEO took the time to email her about how impressed he was with her results. She still has that email today; she was amazed that he took the time to do that for her. She was thrilled and felt even more motivated to continue performing because she knew she was valued. The experience has stayed with her for 10 years so far – so make sure people remember you that way too; it doesn't cost anything to say 'well done and thank you' but it can mean everything.

It's also important here to remember that people are motivated differently.

Some are motivated towards 'avoiding failure'. They want to know what they must do and what to stop doing that might cause them to fail. They can find it difficult to celebrate success for very long and soon want to move on to what other issues/problems they have which might stop their success.

Others, meanwhile, are motivated by everything that will cause them to succeed. They only want to know the positives of what they need to do and do not want to hear the word 'failure' – it's not a word that's in their 'dictionary'. They celebrate success at every opportunity and look for more ways to do that to ensure their future position.

So where are you motivated – 'Towards Success' or 'Avoiding Failure'? How are your team motivated and their people? A team needs to find ways to celebrate success in a way which fits to the team vision and values.

Team Coaching Moment

How do you like to celebrate success as a team?

Put these events in the calendar. Ensure your team cascade that down to their teams and then arrange some 'town hall meetings' or 'whole organisation events' which bring the whole team together as one.

Remember the NHS PCT who did this when it had never been done before? The staff felt included, they felt emotionally connected to the success of the organisation, they become motivated because they were asked for their input, they felt a vital part of the process of that PCT and they 'all' worked together to turn it around from 'failing' to 'performing'.

So it is important to motivate and inspire and then channel the enthusiasm into producing the results.

Ensuring staff/employees are involved early is proven to be an important step to success. You could do this by doing something we call a Perception Study or what is sometimes called a Team Climate Study. This asks the rest of your organisation about you as leaders. It will contain questions like:

- How motivated are you?

- How supported are you?

- How empowered are you?

- How well do you know and understand the vision and values of your leadership team?

· How well do you understand your role and your responsibility to the success of the team?

By finding out what your people think of you as a leadership team you can know what you need to do to improve the culture and performance in your wider team. You can therefore know now what your leadership team need to do differently to change the culture.

Celebrating success is an 'art' – some leaders have to work at it whilst to others it's a necessary part of who they are. Refer to your purpose, vision and values and ask yourself the following questions as a team.

Team Coaching Moment

How can we as a team recognise and reward great performance and success?

How can we celebrate success and ensure it is embedded in our culture?

Make sure that every day it is in the culture running through the DNA of the team – in its spirit.

Don't be like a very well-known ex-leader who only gave negative feedback, only told his people what they were doing wrong and what they must not do. No one felt they could do anything right and that whatever they did would never be enough for him. He would always find 'the flaws' – this led to a demotivated and disengaged board and it also lead to a lack of confidence and self-esteem with the rest of the organisation, and it led to a culture of fear – no one knew exactly what was going on and they were too frightened to say when they did. He was replaced.

So please take the time to be a great leader:

- A leader who is continually open to develop

- A leader who develops their teams

- A leader who celebrates success with their teams

- A leader who is focused on achieving the financial targets and their leadership goals

- Be the leader that makes a positive difference to their people

- Be the leader who inspires them and who they will always remember and aspire to be like

Take the time.

I know you can do it. I know you are unique and that you have the strengths to enable your success. I know you want to be a great leader not just an OK one. I know because you have already started your leadership journey.

Enjoy it, knowing you will make mistakes along the way but every day you will become better and better. You can do it.

'It's not the mountain we have to conquer, but ourselves'
Edmund Hillary

Summary

1. Celebrate success.

2. Give verbal and written recognition – formal and informal.

3. Give positive feedback.

4. Give feed forward.

5. Coach to success.

6. Take time out to socialise.

7. Understand the team's motivations – towards or away from?

8. Implement a Perception Study.

9. Have fun building a great team and your leadership identity.

References

Strategies of Genius – Robert Dilts

Changing beliefs with NLP – Robert Dilts

The Seven Habits of Highly Effective People - Stephen Covey

Now Discover Your Strengths – Marcus Buckingham

Fight Back – Hannah Keep (Available from www.viinternational.com)

NLP at Work – Sue Knight

Strengthsfinder-www.strengthsfinder.com

Strengthscope - www.strengthspartnership.com

ECI 360 - Hay Group – *www.haygroup.com - available through Vi International*

°MBTI°/°FiroB°°/°TKI°°° - available through Vi International or

UK- OPPLtd, Elsfield Hall, 15-17 Elsfield Way, Oxford, OX2 8EP Tel+44 (0)845 603 9958 www.opp.eu.com

USA – CPPInc., 1055 Joaquin Road, 2nd Floor, Mountain View California USA 94043

° FIRO-B is a registered trade mark of CPP, Inc. OPP Ltd is licensed to use the trade mark in Europe

° MBTI, the MBTI logo, Myers-Briggs Type Indicator and Myers-Briggs are registered trade marks of the Myers-Briggs Type Indicator Trust. OPP Ltd is licensed to use the trade marks in Europe

° MBTI is a registered trade mark of the Myers-Briggs Type Indicator Trust. OPP Ltd is licensed to use the trade mark in Europe

° Myers-Briggs is a registered trade mark of the Myers-Briggs Type Indicator Trust. OPP Ltd is licensed to use the trade mark in Europe

° Myers-Briggs Type Indicator is a registered trade mark of the Myers-Briggs Type Indicator Trust. OPP Ltd is licensed to use the trade mark in Europe

Illustrations by Dylan Floyd www.dylanfloyd.co.uk

Nicola McHale

About the Author

Nicola McHale (Ross) has over 20 years of experience as a results-focused Executive Impact Coach, working with global leaders as they drive sensitive transformation. Her success means that they take Nicola with them as they move organisations and roles because they know she makes a significant difference to their success. Her depth of knowledge and extensive experience delivering throughout Europe, Asia and the United States gives her the 'edge' when working with culturally diverse teams.

With an earlier career in the competitive world of fashion, beauty and health in London, New York and Paris, she brings with her an in-depth knowledge of the critical components of personal impact and presence in leadership. Nicola has worked with many prominent leaders to improve their impact to ensure they are prepared for media involvement.

Working alongside presidents, vice-presidents, CEOs and GMs within organisations like American Express, Diageo, Virgin Atlantic, Microsoft and HSBC, Nicola's practical approach and challenging questions provide a team and the individuals with the power to fast-track success throughout their organisation.

With a proven track record and return on investment, every leader and team Nicola works with achieves a significant improvement in their results. Her record of success means that she maintains strong relationships with senior leaders, partnering with them to drive transformation.

With her knowledge and experience, she has probably met every issue a leader has to face and every issue a team will have which could prevent them from succeeding. With that knowledge she can fast-track any team and any leader to success better than most.

This book is the story of how to develop yourself as a leader, transform your team and achieve success built on over 20 years of experience.

Lightning Source UK Ltd.
Milton Keynes UK
UKOW040213040712

195407UK00004B/90/P